FROM THE AUTHOR OF THE HIGHLY ACCLAIMED
PROGRAMMED TEXTS TO LEARN
GUJARATI AND ENGLISH

SANSKRIT

AN APPRECIATION WITHOUT APPREHENSION

Setubandh Language Series Volume : 5

A Programmed Text

Prepared By

BHARAT S. SHAH, M. D.

SETUBANDH PUBLICATIONS
NEW YORK

SANSKRIT : AN APPRECIATION WITHOUT APPREHENSION

First U. S. Edition 2003 (The Writers Collective)
Second U. S. Edition 2004 (Setubandh Publications)

OTHER BOOKS BY BHARAT S. SHAH, M.D.

(For ordering tinformation, please see the end pages)

An Introduction to Jainism

"SAMEEPE" A novel (in Gujarati)

❂   *SETUBANDH LANGUAGE SERIES*   ❂

A Programmed Text to Learn Gujarati (Second Edition).

A Crash Course to Learn The Devanagari Script
(For Hindi, Marathi, and Sanskrit Languages).

A Crash Course to Learn The Gujarati Script.

English For The Grandma And Her Children (in Gujarati)

TO

Lalit Kapasi

Once an Arch Rival

My Friend For Over Fifty Years

Whose Company Made Studying Anything Fun !

पापान्निवारयति योजयते हिताय
गुह्यं च गूहति गुणान्प्रकटीकरोति ।
आपद्गतं च न जहाति ददाति काले
सन्मित्रलक्षणमिदं प्रवदन्ति सन्ताः ॥

*Saves from committing sins, guides into beneficial actions,
Keeps what is worth hiding, proclaims virtues to the world;
Does not abandon in bad times, gives help when needed,
These are the characteristics of a good friend, the sages say !*

PREFACE

*"Sanskrit is deeper than Greek, richer than Latin,
and more sophisticated than either of them."*

-Thomas Macauley, a British scholar.

Maybe it is so. I have not studied either Greek or Latin well enough to testify to the verity or otherwise of the above proclamation. But we do know that its writer was not from India, where Sanskrit is as alive as Greek, and far more than Latin. The latter is sometimes labelled as a "dead language", while Sanskrit is anything but.

Gandhian Gujarati writer Kakasaheb Kalelkar says, *"Thinking of the glowing gem stones of Sanskrit to be burning charcoals, people stay away from them !"* That's indeed a real shame, for several reasons. It is akin to sick people staying away from the medicine they really need.

There are two kinds of people: those who love Sanskrit, and those who are intimidated by it. Those loving it cite innumerable prayers, scriptures, epics, the holy book Gita, the wisdom stored in the Vedas, Upanishads, and in the likes of the Panchatantra. They quote an endless series of their favorite pearls and nuggets from the vast Sanskrit literature. They cannot even for a moment forget the great poet Kalidas, Bhavabhuti, and other prolific writers.

Those who are intimidated, are also fans of Sanskrit, which apparently remains inaccessible to them. For them, it is like a gift so well wrapped, they cannot even open it. Very nuances and beauty become a burden for their eager souls. They are left holding only the burden, and are deprived of the beauty. That's still worse.

A Sanskrit saying goes: *"The beast of burden donkey, even when loaded with sandlewood logs, is aware of only the weight of the load, and not its fragrance!"* The donkey is incapable, and probably unappreciative of the fragrance, but I have met many people my age and younger, who are genuinely interested in Sanskrit, have studied it, maybe "had scored good marks in it on the exams', but have totally lost it now.

A language is only as dead as the people using it. This is not an accusation, nor a put down of anyone. There is a practical reason for this statement. Sanskrit is the mother of all north Indian mother tongues. All of these languages are losing their speakers-base, that is, those who can speak fluently in those tongues, and the loss is being blamed on the powerful influence of the English language and the Western culture. Economic considerations have resulted in the popularity of English-medium schools. When language goes, religion and culture follow.

One thing should be clear. Weeds don't kill the grass lawn, they grow only where the lawn doesn't. North Indian languages replenish their vocabulary with words flowing in from villages, and from city streets. Plus, for technical and sophisticated literature, they draw heavily on Sanskrit, which is still amazingly capable of meeting any demand placed on it. Recently someone suggested that it would make even an excellent computer language.

We have lost all contact with our villages, and our writers have lost contact with our Main Street. Our umbilical cord to Sanskrit is also severed. Now there remains no source of new words to replace the vanishing vocabulary. English is the only language from which new words can come in. In itself that wouldn't be bad. We have borrowed heavily from Persian (Farasi), Urdu, Portugese, Spanish, etc. English has borrowed many Sanskrit and Indian words.

The problem is, English word order is different than that of the north Indian languages. As a result, once you use one English word, you find yourself using a string of them without realizing it. Then we find English to be easy, and our mother tongues and Sanskrit to be difficult. That sets in motion a downward spiral. There is only one way to break it. Brush up our Sanskrit.

There are many who are advocating with fanaticism, re-introducing Sanskrit into our lives. They are similarly trying to stuff local languages down people's throat, without an inkling about why these things did not work in the first place. With friends like these, Sanskrit needs no enemies.

Many Indian families, and those from the West Indies, etc. with an Indian background, have kept up their religious practices (worshiping and other rituals). They chant hymns, say prayers, and conduct wedding and other ceremonies in Sanskrit, and take pains to explain all this to their American friends, or sons- and daughters-in-law, without even themselves having the foggiest idea about what they are perfunctorily going through.

Children and young adults learn computer languages like HTML, C+++, and so on to communicate with the computer in its own language. Despite all their brilliance, they cannot do that with their own mother! Granted, learning a language may be difficult. However, learning its script is not that demanding a pursuit, and it offers great rewards in a very short while.

Sanskrit and its north Indian daughters are phonetic languages, which English certainly is not. A tremendous amount of meager and dwindling resources are squandered in transliterating (poorly, at best) Sanskrit writings into English, which the reluctant students reconstruct and say with creative pronunciations, thereby frustrating both sides irreparably. Only if they would learn the script!

One doesn't have to be a scholar of Sanskrit to understand and appreciate its rich literature. Anybody and everybody can have fun with it. Not all can swim in an ocean, but all can play with the breaking surf. All can be amazed after watching the moon-landing without being a rocket scientist. We have to separate two things quite clearly: Writing original material in Sanskrit is one thing, while reading and appreciating what is already written is something else.

The traditional teaching of Sanskrit appears to aim at making everybody an original writer and scholar of Sanskrit. This is not realistic. It requires a thorough knowledge of Sanskrit grammar, all its nouns with various endings, their genders, numbers, etc. Then the verbs, with their numbers, persons, tenses, ten groups or Ganas, three kinds like Atmanepadi, and so on. Add to this, the innumerable rules of joining letters and words, plus the participles, tens of meters, and the religious and cultural baggage that the content invariably carries. Thank God, the donkey is at least alive to appreciate the burden !

On the other hand, if you are not going to write independently, I believe you can very easily survive without any of the above. This book is written based on that belief, and the remaining pages can vouch for its vindication or otherwise. To appreciate beauty, you need eyes and heart, and once you like something, you will never forget it.

The difference between these two approaches is the difference between apprehension and appreciation. There is absolutely no need for the former, while the latter is a must. Even to share this appreciation, you don't have to be a scholar. For sure, I am not one.. I have not studied formally, any Sanskrit after I left high school. I have admired and appreciated the warmth of the great Sanskrit works from a distance, or at the coattails of the experienced masters.

There are many scholarly books for learning Sanskrit, and any serious student should take advantage of them. I have drawn gratefully upon several of them. Traditional, comprehensive teaching of Sanskrit has its well deserved place. The present, unique and innovative work is only a bridge to those great works, and many more beyond them. Not every good thing has to be painful.

I am thankful to all who have contributed to the successful 15 years of Setubandh Publications. This is the fifth volume in its Language Series. Gujarati and Jainism books are already in their second US editions. All have been published, or are being published in their Indian editions as well.

Acknowledgements:

This book was already completely written way back in 1989, and my daughter Manisha had, in a bout of enthusiasm typed up its first 15 pages. It stayed in exile for the last 12 years of no fault of its own. Although Setubandh has managed to succeed against all odds and prognostications, the sad fact remains that writing, type-setting, financing, and selling educational books, no matter how worthwhile or badly needed they may be, is a discouraging misadventure.

Our enthusiasm for making and keeping our next generation totally immersed in Indian culture is waning, and has practically disappeared with our children getting married. Marriage is the panacea for all our problems. A married person does not need to know his or her mother tongue, religion, or culture! Selling one book every few weeks in such environment is not the best way to recover the inventory cost of tens of thousands of dollars "invested" in every title published.

Why all this under "acknowledgements"? The Apple Computer Co. introduced the true desktop publishing in 1984, enabling people like myself to work without the help of established publishers, most of whom are in the business for making a buck for themselves. Printing fewer than 2000 copies is prohibitively expensive, and looking at those 2000 books sitting in the garage obviates the need for a shrine of the goddess of learning, Saraswati.

The next revolution started in 2000, and that was the best thing that happened since desktop publishing. It was the acceptance and popularization of Print On Demand publishing. In that system, the book exists only as a computer file, and it is printed out literally one copy at a time as needed, thereby getting rid of the inventory outlays and consequent frustrations. The costs are still substantial, but maybe one tenth of what they used to be, for an experienced publisher like Setubandh.

I am grateful to the Writers Collective, its Director Ms.Lisa Grant, and the Fidlar Doubleday Press for publishing this book.I cannot forget the interminable chain of e-mails exchanged across the Atlantic with Ms. Samantha Wall to discuss the attractive cover, draping the book.

Now quality books can be prepared and sold without one's losing sleep over whether, when, and who will buy them. Another fringe benefit is lower costs, which are reflected in Setubandh's ability to maintain the lower sale prices despite inflation. Before knowledge can liberate anyone, the knowledge itself has to be liberated. I think that's what is happening now. And I am thankful for that.

To find free time, or rather to carve out a chunk of it from busy schedules is another problem. I would like to thank my son Nikhil and daughter in law Lori for their meticulous proof reading. I can never forget Prof. Madhusudan Kapadia's encouragement, help, guidance, and blessings, together with his providing some of the material included here, especially for sections on Meters and on Figures of Speech, plus his thorough critical review of the typescript.

Prof. C. L. Shashtri, once my wife Usha's professor of Sanskrit at the St. Xavier's College in Ahmedabad, and an author of several highly regarded college level text books of Sanskrit, was kind enough to go over the entire work. I am especially thankful to him, because this work may amount to a blasphemy of the classical way of teaching Sanskrit.

I am gratefully appreciative of my wife Usha for, not only being a desciple of Prof. Shashtri, and for surviving a liver transplant nearly four years ago, but also for facilitating my working on one misadventure after another, without my having any apprehension on that account.

-Bharat S. Shah, M.D.
Great Neck, NY.
April 2003.

8

Where is the Table of Contents?

This is a programmed text, which takes the reader through the course one step at a time, making sure that the reader understands each step before going further. The topics are introduced and explained in a friendly style, but not in any conventional order. Therefore programmed texts do not always have a formal Table of Contents in the beginning. The entire text is to be read from beginning to end. The back pages contain directions to the particular topic that the reader may want to return to.

Having said that, I *have* included a Table of Contents just for scholars, reviewers, and others who are familiar with Sanskrit, and may want to know what topics are covered in this book. However, the student is well advised not to look at it at all, and thereby not to be intimidated by it.

Moreover, some words in the Contents would have to be listed in Sanskrit, which the reader is not yet expected to be familiar with. Plus, looking at the Contents in itself can be quite intimidating, even though the actual text may not be. There is nothing conventional about this book, although it does respect the previous great teachers and scholars, and stands in awe before their contributions.

This book is organized in four parts, each devoted to a progressively higher level of material. It works to remove fear generated by dreaded topics, and guides the reader through previously painful parts with gentle fun. Finally, it is hoped, the reader will emerge with confidence, understanding, and an appreciation of Sanskrit.

Part: I.   This part deals in an innovative way with the Devanagari alphabet, including the consonants, vowels, vowel symbols, conjoined characters, numerals, and punctuation marks. It runs through pages 1-61.

Part: II.   This is the main body of the text. In an extremely painless and pleasurable manner, it takes the reader comfortably through the generally fearsome aspects of learning Sanskrit. There is nothing to memorize, no tedious rules and exceptions to struggle through, not getting all tangled up in nouns, cases, gender, number, etc., or the verbs, with their tenses, persons, participles, and what not. Student emerges from this section, well conversant with the charming way in which the language operates. It runs from p. 63-159.

Part: III.   This part takes the reader into heretofore avoided, delightful sections of the Sanskrit grammar, without ever realizing it. This section contains many power tools, getting the student all dressed up for the party to follow. This part extends from page 161-215.

Part: IV.   This is the Treasure Chest, for which this journey was undertaken. There is minimal direct teaching here. It is all sheer fun, unbelievable and until now, buried under various rules and exceptions. It acquaints the student with lyrical Sanskrit meters, and figures of speech adorning the language. It ends with about 100 pearls or gems of Sanskrit poetry, philosophy, prayers, and wisdom. It spans the pages 217-270.

Glossary: There is none. My experience (with my books to learn Gujarati, English, and on Jainism) tells me that the Glossary is the least used, and the most labor intensive part, generally adding only some dead weight, and increasing the printing costs and the sale price. There are many excellent dictionaries available.

Index: Again, there is none. The part: IV contains many references to the appropriate text pages, adequate for searching the text for a particular verse or a part of it.

The end pages contain information

on this and other books from Bharat S. Shah, M.D.

TABLE OF CONTENTS

Dedication
Preface
Where is the Table of Contents?
Table of Contents

Part: I. The Devanagari Alphabet

1.	Introduction		1
	a.	Vowels and their symbols	7
	b.	Vowels without a symbol	11
	c.	Creating vowels with symbols	12
	d.	Meet the Devanagari alphabet	14
2.	**Devanagari equivalents of English characters (Table)**		**16**
3.	The rest of the alphabet		19
	a.	Consonants joined together	22
	b.	Special characters	25
	c.	A special way of writing	27
	d.	Special letters	28
	e.	Punctuation marks	29
	f.	Numerals, fractions, decimals	30
4.	More about the alphabet		
	a.	Review and practice	32
		i. Writing in Devanagari	38
		ii. Similar, not same	39
		iii. Transliteration and translation	42
		iv. Together or apart?	44
		v. Bite your tongue	45
	b.	Practice, practice, practice!	46
		i. One less sign to worry about	47
		ii. The more the merrier	48
		iii. Aspiring to learn	49
		iv. The third half	50
		v. A curse in disguise!	52
	c.	**English equivalents of Devanagari characters (Table)**	**54**
		i. Vowels and symbols	55
		ii. Special symbols	55

5.	Alphabetical order		55
	i.	Everything in its proper place	57
	ii.	Cut that out!	60
6.	Conclusion Part: I		61

Part: II. The Fabric of Sanskrit

7.	Introduction		63
8.	Changeless words		65
9.	Nouns: cases		66
	a.	Singular and plural numbers	66
10.	Sanskrit words		
	a.	in English	68
	b.	in daily life	69
11.	Nouns:		
	a.	Second (objective) case	74
	b.	Third case	75
	c.	All cases	77
12.	Nouns:		
	a.	Ram	79
	b.	Hari	80
	c.	Sons and daughters	81
13.	Verbs: persons		82
14.	Sanskrit word order		83
15.	Pronouns: personal		85
16.	Nouns: Effect of gender: Nouns vis a vis verbs		87
17.	Verbs: Ten groups		91
18.	Changeless words, more about them		92
19.	Parts of speech		92
20.	Nouns:		
	a.	Numbers: Dual	96
	b.	Piled up words	98

21.	Union of adjacent vowels			100
22.	Nouns: Declensions:			
	a.	Ram		102
	b.	Van		104
	c.	Nouns: Cases:		
		i.	Fourth	106
		ii.	Seventh	109
23.	Union of			
	a.	Vowels (contd)		111
	b.	Words		112
24.	Adjectives: Agreement			113
25.	Union of Visarga			116
26.	Nasal consonants and sign (Anuswar)			120
27.	Prefixes for nouns and verbs			121
28.	Nouns: Cases: Examples			
	a.	Veer		126
	b.	Ram		128
29.	Pronouns, personal			130
30.	Verbs: Types			133
31.	Adjectives made by joining words			134
32.	Unions of			
	a.	Words (Samas)		141
	b.	Vowels		142
	c.	Consonants		142
	d.	Visarga		142
33.	Nouns:			
	a.	Declensions of "Sita"		149
	b.	Declensions of "Guru"		147
	c.	Endings A, Aa, and U		148
34.	Verbs:			
	a.	Conjugations of "To Go"		149
	b.	Groups (Ten)		151
	c.	Conjugations of "To Be"		152
	d.	Conjugations of "To Gain"		153
	e.	Second person		154
35.	Conclusion Part: II			159

Part: III. Advanced. Using the Power Tools

36.	General	161
	a. Adjectives	
	b. Cardinal and Ordinal numbers	165
	c. Fractions	167
37.	Indo-European languages	168
	a. Sir William Jones	169
38.	Participles	172
39.	Verbs: Remaining groups	176
40.	Nouns:	
	a. Vowel endings	178
	b. Consonant endings	179
	c. "Ri" ending	181
41.	Degrees of comparison	
	a. Adjectives	185
	b. Verbs	186
42.	Pronouns:	190
	a. Personal pronouns	
	i. Singular	191
	(1) First Person	193
	ii. Plural	194
	(1) Second Person	196
	(2) Third Person	198
	b. Other pronouns	200
43.	Verbs	
	a. Tenses	203
	i. Future tense	204
	ii. Present tense	204
	iii. Past tense	206
	(1) Negative prefix	206
	b. Voices	207
	i. active	208
	ii. passive	208
	c. Moods	208
44.	Prepositions	211
	a. Using the seventh case	211

45.	Conjunctions and Interjections		213
46.	Conclusion part: III		215

Part: IV. The Treasure Chest

47.	The Treasure Chest		217
	a.	The Good Sayings	218
	b.	Alternate Indian National Anthem	228
	c.	Prayers	
		i. School prayer	229
		ii. Supreme being	230
		iii. Lord Ganesha	230
		iv. Saraswati	230
		v. Jinas	231
		vi. Lord Vishnu	232
		vii. Lord Krishna	232
		viii. Lord Krishna (Child)	232
		ix. Laxmi, the mother earth	233
48.	Immeasurable pleasure		235
	a.	Meters	236
	b.	Figures of Speech	252

Part: V. Index

49.	Verses that you already know		265
	a.	Verses from the text parts I - III	265
	b.	First-line index of the Treasure Chest	269
		i. Meters	269
		ii. Figures of speech	270
50.	Conclusion of Sanskrit: An Appreciation Without Apprehension		270

Ordering information   271-4

··

Part: I
THE DEVANAGARI ALPHABET

··

Congratulations! You have started to study a very interesting and fascinating language, which is famous for its vast literature. It is the language of Hindu religious books, and of many classics. The epics - Ramayan and Mahabharat - are originally in Sanskrit. You may have read stories from the Pancha-tantra, which is also in Sanskrit.

If you are from Northern India, your mother tongue is derived from Sanskrit. If your mother tongue is Marathi, or Hindi, then you might like to know that these two languages even share the same written alphabet, called Devanagari ("of the city of gods") alphabet, or script.

☞ Sanskrit is written in the *Devanagari* script.

Other North Indian languages, viz. Bengali, Gujarati, etc. use somewhat modified characters, but the alphabet is the same. The South Indian languages, viz., Tamil, Telugu, Kannada and Malayalum are not closely related to Sanskrit, but their alphabet contains the same sounds in the same order. The words are unrelated to Sanskrit. However, many South Indian names are in Sanskrit.

Thus, Sanskrit is the mother of most of our Indian mother tongues! It is not in common use today, but it is far from being a dead language. Not only that, it is a very lively language. There are a few scholars who can write and speak in Sanskrit. As a matter of fact, you or your parents may know several prayers that are, you guessed it right, in Sanskrit.

This is a Programmed Text. It is interactive. We will talk to each other throughout. You will not be judged, and there will be no exam. I will introduce one topic after another. At every juncture, I will ask you one or more questions. You are not required to know the answers.

This system allows you to pat yourself on the back, if you already know the material. If you do not know, then it teaches you right then and there. All steps are linked, and their sequence is meticulously arranged as a program. This is how it works.

You may have already noticed the wide right margin. I am writing this on the left side. Whenever there is any question that you should try to answer, there will be an arrow like this: (→) pointing towards the right margin. The arrow indicates that there is something written there, mostly the answer to the question just asked.

You should keep the right margin covered with your hand, or with a 2.5 x 11" card board. After trying to answer the question, uncover only the portion of the right margin containing the answer. Answer the questions either verbally, or write the answers on a separate sheet of paper.

Do not just read through with the right margin exposed, or else you will miss all the fun, and lose credit for knowing the answers. There is a reason why I went through a lot of work to prepare this program to help you along. Don't let a little laziness destroy it.

Before we go on, let me ask you, how did you get interested in learning Sanskrit?

2

Read the following and check one or more reasons that apply to you:

☐ Sanskrit is the language of hymns and prayers.

☐ I have heard so many good sayings ("Subhashitani"), beautiful couplets, verses, lovely quotable quotes, that I would like to learn many more.

☐ I know my North Indian mother tongue already (Bravo!) and learning Sanskrit will improve my control over my mother tongue.

☐ I have studied Latin/Greek, and would like to study the Indian classical language.

☐ I like Sanskrit "Shloka"s (They are stanzas of Sanskrit poems. You will learn many good ones).

☐ I have seen and read Sanskrit writings written in English (i.e. transliterated into English), but I found these to be quite difficult to follow. Therefore I decided to study Sanskrit.

Now, cover the right margin, and keep it covered from now on. Any and all of the reasons given above are valid reasons to study Sanskrit. You may be able to think of a few more. List them here:

→ 1.
2.
3.

Thank you. Whatever your reason(s) is/are to undertake this study, I hope you will be able to enjoy your adventure. I will do my best to help you, and make it as simple and interesting as possible.

Do you know that Sanskrit and English are related to each other?

→ Yes. They both are members of a family of languages, called

3

"Indo-European languages".

There are lots of similarities between English and Sanskrit. You will pick up many similar words as you study more, but the similarity between the languages themselves is important to us now.

☞ Just as with English, and unlike Urdu, Sanskrit is also written from left to right, and from top to bottom.

The differences are also interesting, but these can wait for now. I will point out the important differences as we come across them.

THE DEVANAGARI ALPHABET

First, let us go over the alphabet. Even if you know the Devanagari alphabet, I would urge you to read on, rather than skipping this and the next chapters. That will provide you with a good review, and help you pick up a few points. You will also discover an innovative way to teach the Devanagari alphabet and Sanskrit to someone else.

The Devanagari alphabet has very little in common with the English alphabet, but it offers several advantages to us. For one, each letter (a,b,c,d) can be pronounced in one and only one way. In English, the letter "U" is pronounced differently in the words like But, Put, Busy, Tongue, Debut, etc. Its Sanskrit counterpart would always be pronounced as in Put.

☞ In Devanagari alphabet, each letter (a,b,c,d) can be pronounced in one and only one way.

4

In addition, each letter carries a horizontal line on top of it. I know you cannot yet read Devanagari, but this is what it looks like:

संस्कृत <u>ENGLISH</u>

Where are the English letters written, above the line or below?

→ Above

And Devanagari?

→ Below

☞ English letters are written above the line, while Devanagari letters are written below the line.

What is common among all Devanagari letters?

→ They all have a horizontal line at the top.

I should mention that Devanagari numerals do not have such a line at the top. They are written the same way as the English ones, but below the line.

☞ Devanagari numerals, unlike letters, do not have a line at the top.

We can start with a numeral. We have to start from nothing, or zero. In Devanagari, you write "0" (zero) the same way as you do in English. "Well, finally we saw something civilized!" you may say.

→ You are correct. "Sanskrit" means "civilized".

Would you like to guess why "zero" is written in the same way in both the languages?

5

→ Because "zero" was invented in India. The Western world got it through the Arabs, hence the "Arabic" numerals, as opposed to the Roman ones (I, V, X, C, L, etc.) without a zero.

So, what is the contribution of India towards civilization?

→ Zero !

Before you start making fun, let me ask you, do you know any sweet sounding word in English that comes from Sanskrit?

→ "Candy" from the Sanskrit word "Khand" meaning "a chunk"

So, a "sweet candy" comes from a "sweet chunk" ! Some of you may have tasted the Indian sweet dish called "Shrikhand" ("sweet chunk"). Sanskrit has given many religious and philosophical ideas to the world.

Do you know any other words in English that have come from Sanskrit?

→ Nirvana (Salvation), Swastika (a four-pronged symbol)

Any more words?

→ Brahmin (a teacher, a scholar), Pundit (an expert, a scholar), Guru (a teacher).

In English, the words "Brahmin", "Guru", and "Pundit" are often used in a somewhat derogatory manner, as a put-down, but in Sanskrit these words convey a lot of respect.

6

Vowels and Vowel Symbols:

Let us begin with the word 'America'. Since we would prefer to have only one letter represent only one sound, and because 'C' conveys 'S' sound (Nice), and also a 'K' sound (Cut, Car), let us replace 'C' with 'K', thus: Amerika. In this word, there are two 'a's, the first, and the last letters, and both are pronounced differently. We will underline the second (last) 'a', thus: Amerik<u>a</u>.

'A' sound as in 'alone', 'American Indian'
'<u>A</u>' sound as in 'c<u>ar</u>', 'F<u>ar</u>'

In Devanagari, instead of writing out the whole vowels (A, E, I, O, U) after each consonant, we use their symbols. The symbol for '<u>a</u>' is a vertical line like this: ा. It follows the letter: ■ा (where the box ■ is any letter of the alphabet).

☞ Note that the horizontal line at the top of all letters is characteristic of the Devanagari script.

Amerik<u>a</u>	becomes	→	A me ri k ा
C<u>ar</u>	becomes	→	K ा r
B<u>ar</u>	becomes	→	B ा r

Similarly, the vowel symbol for 'I' (as in 'India') is ि■ and it goes before the letter. The 'ri' in 'Amerika' will become ि r :

Amerika	becomes	→	A me ि r k ा
Mita	becomes	→	ि M t ा
Gira	becomes	→	ि G r ा

7

We can replace 'e' with an inverted check mark over the letter (■), to change 'me' in America into m̂ and

Ame͡rkⁱ	becomes	→	A m̂ ͡rkⁱ
Patel	becomes	→	Pa t̂ l

If you put a slightly modified f̂■ behind a letter thus ■î, then you get 'ee' sound:

Geeta	→	Gî tî
Meet	→	Mî t

Just as f̂■ and ■î for 'I' and 'EE' go before and after a letter, the symbols for 'U' and 'OO' both go under it. The symbol for 'U' is ▮ and for 'OO' is ▮. For example:

Put	→	B̤ t
Roof	→	R̤ f
Booth	→	R̤ th
Bush	→	B̤ sh

And to refresh your memory, write these:

Bath	→	Bⁱ th
Bit	→	f̂B t
Beet	→	Bî t

In English, there are five basic vowels, viz. A, E, I, O, U. Of these, we did not cover 'O' yet. For 'O' we do not need any new symbol, but will combine two symbols we already know: ■ī and ■.

Hold	→	Hī̀ ld
Pole	→	Pī̀ le
Polo	→	Pī̀ Lī̀

There are some less frequently used combinations. Instead of one inverted check mark, we can use two:

■	and	■ī	instead of	■	and	■ī
'Ai'	and	'Au'	instead of	'E'	and	'O'

Jain	J̀ n	(Does not rhyme with PAIN).
Vaishnav	V̀ shna v	
Kailas	K̀ la s	
Gautama	G̀ī ta ma	
Aurangzeb	À ī ran g z̀ b	(The last Moghul emperor)

Note that 'Au' is not pronounced as in 'Automobile.' It is 'A' (the first 'A' in 'America') and 'U' (as in 'Put') said in rapid sequence. 'Ai' is 'A' and 'I' (as in 'India') said in rapid sequence.

☞ It is better to ask someone to show you how to pronounce 'Ai' and 'Au,' because in English these sound are not used.

A dot on the top of a letter, ■ indicates the nasal 'UM' or 'UN' sound. Now, see these words:

Aurangzeb	Aͨ r g z b
Hunt	H t
Hunch	H ch
Apartment	A pͭ rt m t
Dentist	D tͭ st
Lint	Lͭ t

Try to read the following:

Aͦ K L   →   (Uncle)

Aͭ Tͭ   →   (Auntee)

A Mͭ   →   (Uma)

Aͭ G L   →   (Eagle)

The next and the last symbol, which is extremely commonly used in Sanskrit, looks like a colon (:) and is put after a letter ■: to indicate breathing out completely saying 'oh' or 'ah,' etc.

P:	P-H		Pͭ:	Pa-Ha
P:	Pu-Hu		Pͭ:	Po-Ho

That concludes our vowel symbols. Let me list them for you:

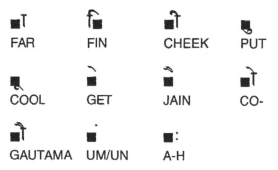

■ͭ	■	■ͭ	■
FAR	FIN	CHEEK	PUT
■	■	■	■ͭ
COOL	GET	JAIN	CO-
■ͭ	■	■:	
GAUTAMA	UM/UN	A-H	

The last two symbols actually do not represent any vowels, but they are tagged on after other vowel symbols.

Let me point out to you again that these symbols save a lot of time and trouble. Instead of writing out the vowels A, I, EE, U, OO, E, AI, O, AU after each and every consonant, we just write these symbols. Moreover, a simple little dot on top of a letter replaces so many 'M' and 'N's. The best is yet to come!

Vowel With No Symbol:

Read these words (never mind their meaning for now):

Bharat	Raman	Saral
Manan	Nayan	Charan
Dhaval	Gaman	

We used 43 characters to write these words (I counted them for you) in English, of which there are 27 consonants, and 16 vowels. 16 out of 43 is 37%. In Devanagari, we drop all such 'A' sounds altogether. That is a nearly 40% saving in labor right there. We use no symbol for this 'A' sound. No symbol means A, as the first 'A' in 'America'.

☞ In Devanagari, no symbol is used to represent "A" (the first "A" in America)

Take the words listed above. In Devanagari, we write all these words as shown below (without the spaces between the letters):

BH R T	R M N	S R L
M N N	N Y N	CH R N
DH V L	G M N	

11

So, now you know how to write in Devanagari, using the English alphabet and Devanagari vowel symbols with any letter.

Now, let us try these with a consonant like "M" to indicate the vowel sounds

M Mा ीM Mी M M
M M Mो Mौ M M:

It works the same way with any other consonant like P, Z, G, T, D, etc. With consonants (i.e., letters other than A, E, I, O, U) we use symbols for vowels. These symbols are never used alone, by themselves, without a consonant.

☞ The vowel symbols are never used without a consonant.

Creating More Vowels By Using Symbols:

For using the vowels themselves as letters, we use the forms of 'A'. The basic vowel 'A' (the first...) is written thus: अ.

Try to write the letter अ with vowel symbols:

→ अ आ इि अी
अु अू अे अै
ओ औ अं अ:

However, for convenience (certainly not yours), a few of the vowels are written in a different way, e.g.,

इ	is written as	इ
ई	"	ई
अु	"	उ
अू	"	ऊ
ए	"	ए
ऐ	"	ऐ

The last two above can be very confusing. Look at these carefully. ए has no inverted check mark on top, unlike in ऎ. ऐ has only one, instead of the two we see in ऍ. The vowel series, therefore, looks like this:

Look at the chain of twelve symbols above. This chain is called BARAKSHARI or BARAKHADI (literally, 'a chain of twelve letters'), pronounced as Bī Rī KH Dī.

It is very important to understand when to use the symbols, and when to use the various forms of letter अ as shown above. Let us see a few examples.

Write these in Devanagari or English script (mixed):

America		→	अ м̆ſRKſ
India		→	ई ſDYſ
Indiana		→	ई ſDYſNſ
England		→	ई̆ GL D
Overpass		→	ओ̆VRPſS
Israel		→	ई̆ZRई̆L
Andy		→	ए D̆ी
Airavat	(Divine elephant with seven tusks)	→	ऐRſVT
Arab		→	आRB

As you can see, the same symbols are used to modify the consonants, and also to modify the basic vowel अ to generate other vowels. In other words, various forms of consonants and various vowels are generated by using the same symbols, in the same manner.

☞ Symbols are used with consonants, or with the basic vowel अ in the same manner.

Meet the Devanagari Alphabet:

Believe it or not, you are ready to write in Devanagari now, using the Devanagari alphabet. You may or may not know any Sanskrit words. First, write your own name, those of your family members, your friends, or significant others, using vowel symbols and English consonants.

Write:

Your name	BHARAT	→
Father's name	SHANTILAL	→
Mother's name	KANTABEN	→
Any name	USHA	→

Now, write those names breaking them up into their syllables like this:

BHA RA T	→
SHAN TI LA L	→
KAN TA BE N	→
U SHA	→

Now write them using the symbols, and Devanagari letters that you may know:

BH R T	→
SHĪTTLĪL	→
KĪTĪBN	→
ƷSHĪ	→

Now there are two options:

1.   If it is possible, ask your parents or someone else familiar with Sanskrit, to show you how to write only the letters of your name in Devanagari. Just the letters, not the whole name. Say, your name is KOKILA (a girl's name), then ask them to show you K and L only. Then you fill in the symbols for O, I and A.

2.   If there is no such easily accessible help, I have provided on the next page a list of Devanagari equivalents of English alphabet. You may look up and find the letters needed to write all the names on your list.

15

DEVANAGARI EQUIVALENTS OF ENGLISH CHARACTERS

A	अ, आ, ■, ■ा		
B	ब	Bh भ	
C	स (Cycle)	Ch च	Chh छ
	क (Cycle)		
D	द, ड	Dh ध, ढ	
E	■े, ए	EE ■ी, ई, अी	
F/Ph	फ	G ज (George, "Jyo")	Jh झ
		ग (God)	Gh घ
H	ह		
I	ि■, अि, इ	EE ■ी, अी, ई	
J	ज	Jh/z झ	
K	क	Kh ख	
L	ल	L/R ळ	
M	म, ■ं	N न, ण, ■ं	
O	■ो, ओ	OO ■ू, ऊ, अू	
P	प	Ph/F फ	Qu क्व
R	र	R/L ळ	
S	स	SH श, ष	
T	त (Et tu!)	Th थ (Theme, Theory)	
		ध (The, Then)	
	ट (Brute?)	ठ ('Total' said as 'Thothal')	
U	■ु, उ, अु	OO ■ू, ऊ, अू	
V/W	व	X(KS) क्ष (KSH)	
Y	य	Z/Jh झ	

16

Feel free to refer to this list as you go along. You will remember these by practice. I will write a few names here, and you may want to write a few more. Since I don't know your name, let us begin with mine. My name is BHARAT. We will write it like this: Bh R T.

There are several sounds like Bh, Ph, Gh, Dh, Th, etc. that are written in English as two letters, B and h, and so on. In Devanagari, they are indeed represented by only one letter. Let us also treat them as one letter.

Bh R T	is	Bharat
Dh Nî	is	Dhani (a girl's name)
Ghî Rî	is	Ghari (a sweet)
Aî Dhî R	is	Adhar (a support)
िPh Lî Sî Phî	is	Philosophy

Soon, I will stop writing the English pronunciations. You can check the list to find that—

Bh   is written as   भ

R   "   र

T   "   त   (also as ट. That's why it is better to ask).

So, we write my name as भरत. We did not need any vowel symbols here. But suppose we want to write BHARATI, a girl's name. Then we need to use the vowel symbols:

17

BHARATI → Bhा R तो → भारती

USHA → अ Shा → अुषा
(उषा)

UMA → अ Mा → अुमा
(उमा)

NIKHIL → नि ख़ि L → निखिल

MANISHA → M Nी Shा → मनीषा

PIYUSH → पि Y Sh → पियूष

As for the consonants, you already know ten of them, viz. BH, R, T, M, N, SH, KH, L, Y, and P written as भ, र, त, म, न, ष, ख, ल, य and प respectively, in Devanagari. You may be able to use them in writing the names from your list, or you may need more letters. Even if you do only one or two names every day, you will know the entire Devanagari alphabet (all 36 letters) pretty soon.

☞ Note the horizontal line at the top of all consonants and vowels, and of the vowel symbols touching the top line: म, न, ष, अ, ई, ■ा, ि■ and ■ो.

The Rest of the Alphabet:

Learn the rest of the alphabet slowly, at your own pace. Since you may have a very limited vocabulary in Sanskrit, if any at all, at first you may practice writing English words in Devanagari script.

Devanagari is a phonetic alphabet, unlike English. Therefore, you can write any English word in Devanagari. You never have to guess its pronunciation. One piece of advice.

☞ Follow the sound, not the spelling!

Uncle	is	अंकल,	not	अुंकल
			or	उंकल

But	„	बट,	not	बुट
Kid	„	किड	„	कईड
The	„	ध or धी		

Before we go further, try to write a few words that you already know:

America	→ अमेरिका
Russia	→ रशिया
London	→ लंडन

Devanagari	→ देवनागरी
Ganesh (Lord Ganesh)	→ गणेश

Total	→ टोटल
Ramesh (a boy's name)	→ रमेश

Using the letters you already know, you may try to write a few English words. Try the following:

Paris	→	You try it, please!
Rio De Janero	→	
Natavarlal	→	
Yashavant	→	
Kamini	→	O.K. Read on.

You should have no trouble reading the following words:

नटवरलाल	→	See below.
यशवंत	→	
पेरिस	→	
रीयो डी जानेरो, रीयो डी हेनेरो	→	
कामिनी	→	These are the same words that I asked you to write in the previous paragraph! I will show you soon, how to write "Paragraph".

Let us write a few more words:

Jagat (World)	→	जगत
Jel (a jail), to gel	→	जेल
Chair	→	चेर
Bazaar (Market place)	→	बाझार
Mahesh	→	महेश
Hawaii	→	हवाई

Write:

Ghar	(a house)	→	घर
Vagh	(a tiger)	→	वाघ
Bagh	(a tiger)	→	बाघ
Bag	(rhymes with <u>Ba</u>ptism.		
	A garden)	→	बाग

We are almost done. You probably thought we would never finish.

Let us write

Thought	→	थोट
Thick	→	थिक्र
Think	→	थिंक्र

The next letter ठ is also 'Th', but not as in 'Think', or in 'The'. When you say 'Total' very harshly, like 'Thothal', you are close. Similarly, ढ is also 'Dh', but not like in 'The'. It sounds like a harshly said 'Damn', i.e. 'Dhem'. It is a sound that is unique to Sanskrit. To approximate it, retroflex your tongue, don't let it touch the back of your teeth, and say ड (D) harshly, while breathing out.

ढाका	Dhaka	(Capital of Bangladesh)
ढेल	Dhel	(a pea-hen)
ढोल	Dhol	(a drum)

Just a few more letters to go. फ is very easy. It is 'F' or 'Ph'. We Indians do not discriminate between the two. The same for 'V' and 'W' as well.

☞ In Devanagari, F and PH, as well as V and W, are treated as the same.

Try to write:

Philosophy	→ फिलोसोफी
Joseph	→ जोसेफ
Fine	→ फाईन
Hala (a plow)	→ हळ

In 'Hala' above, both 'a's are अ, and not आ. The letter ळ has a peculiar pronunciation. It is between 'R' and 'L', or र and ल. Try to say 'R' and then 'L'. Note where the tongue touches the palate. Now move the tongue to a position between the two, and say ळ. If you cannot, you can say 'ल' for now. No word begins with ळ. It is rarely used.

There are two more letters with which no words begin. Unlike ळ, they are not even generally written. They are ङ and ञ ('Ung' and 'Yn'). Both are nasal sounds. They are ghost letters. Let us see how to write "Ghost".

Consonants Joined Together (For better or for worse)!

Sometimes two or more letters (consonants) are joined together without a vowel ('conjoined consonants'), as in GHO<u>ST</u>, RI<u>SK</u>, DU<u>MPSTE</u>R, BHA<u>SK</u>AR, <u>SM</u>ITA in which the underlined consonants are joined together without a vowel. If your list contains any names like that, for the time being you can add अ and break up the conjoined ones as follows:

SMITA → S िM T ा → समिता
(Sa MI TA)

BHASKAR → BH ा S K R → भासकर
(BHA SA KA R)

MRIDULA → M R ी ड L ा → मरीदुला
(MA RI DU LA)

Now, you know a few more letters, viz. स, क, र, and द for 'S', 'K', 'R', and 'D' respectively. But SA MI TA is not Smita, and BHA SA KA R is not Bhaskar.

We want to join स + म, स + क, म + र. Both these letters, स and म, contain a vertical line to your right (स is र + ा). We simply drop that line, and then join the remaining with the consonant that follows it.

स मि ता → स् मिता → स्मिता
(स्म is one letter)

भा स क र → भास् कर → भास्कर

व त स ला → वत् सला → वत्सला

Historically, there was a vowel written as ऋ and is now used to convey 'RI' sound (no ■ी to follow. Not श्री, but ऋ), and its remnants show up very commonly as ■ or ■̒ to indicate the half 'R' sound.

पा र व ती → पा ■̒ व ती → पार्वती (Parvati)

श र ट → श ■̒ ट → शर्ट (a shirt)

क रु ष ण → क ■ ष ण → कृष्ण,

not कृष्णा

(Lord Krishna)

म री दु ला→ ■ ■ दु ला → मृदुला (Mridula)
(a girl's name)

☞ Note that ■̒ is part of a vowel. It is used only with consonants, and not with other vowels. There is no "R" sound in ई (अी).

Add to your list the vowel (ऋ), and consonants क, ण, श, व, and ट. Are you able to write all, or any, of the names on your list? Maybe, you need a few more letters.

Write all the vowels and their symbols:

अ	आ	इ	ई
■	■ा	ि■	■ी

उ	ऊ	ए	ऐ
■	■	■े	■ै

ओ	औ	अं	अः
■ो	■ौ	■ं	■ः

| ऋ (Ri) | | ■ | ■̒ |

The letters like क, ट, र, etc. have no vertical lines built into their right end. So, they are physically attached to the next consonants, if a conjoined consonant is needed.

	क त (K T)	क्त	(KT) (No vertical line)
but,	त स (T S)	त्स	(TS) (Vertical line dropped)
	स ट (S T)	स्ट	(ST) (Vertical line dropped)
and	त क (T K)	त्क	(TK) (Vertical line dropped)

You should be able to write these:

Delhi   → दिल्ही

Saraswati (goddess of learning) → सरस्वती

Ghost   → घोस्ट

Moscow   → मोस्को

Fortunate   → फोर्च्युनेट

Special Characters:

Over hundreds of years, several pairs of conjoined consonants have undergone changes because of frequent writings and inevitable evolution. Some of them have evolved into special characters, in which the original individual members may not be easily recognizable. A conjoined pair is treated as one letter.

In the following special characters, the first letter is halved, that is, its vowel is removed.

Try to identify the consonants that are joined:

पत्र	(Patr)	A letter	→	त	+	र
प्रेम	(Prem)	Love	→	प	+	र
श्री.	(Shri)	Mr.	→	श	+	र
श्रीमती	(Shrimati)	Mrs.				
ट्राम	(Tram)	Tram	→	ट	+	र
पार्ट	(Part)	Part, and so on.				
कृष्ण	(Krishn)	Lord Krishna				
हृदय	(Hriday)	Heart	→	ह	+	●
तृप्ति	(Tripti)	Satisfaction				
पद्म	(Padm)	Lotus	→	द	+	म
सह्य	(Sahy)	Bearable	→	ह	+	य

Write the following:

Sentence	→ सेन्टेन्स
Evaluation	→ इवेल्युएशन
Paragraph	→ पेरेग्राफ
Savitri (a mythological woman's name)	→ सावित्री

   If any of the names in your list contain such characters, learn to write them as such. That's life! You and I cannot stop evolution. Eventually you will learn them, too. They are fun, and kind of cute.

A Special Way of Writing:

Many of the special characters shown above came about thanks to an old tradition of writing half letters literally on the top of the complete letter that follows them. Depending upon the typeface (fonts) used in printing, these special characters may or may not be easy to identify.

Whenever any such letter is not clear enough, I have tried to avoid using it in this book. However, you should be able to recognize them.

Half				
ह	+	ऋ	=	हृ
ह		म		ह्म
ह		न		ह्न
ह		य		ह्य →

(Gujarati font, for demonstration only. The Devanagari character would have a horizontal line at the top)

द	द	द
द	व	द्व
द	ऋ	दृ
द	र	द्र
द	ध	द्ध
द	म	द्म

न	न	न, न्न
च	च	च्च
ट	ट	ट्ट
ळ	ळ	ळ्ळ

27

श   च   श्र
श   व   श्व   →   (As above)

Special Letters:

There are two more letters of the alphabet, that are actually not basic, but are in fact, conjoined consonants, and have evolved as special characters. The first one represents the "KSH" sound, as the last "X" in "Xerox".

अ क श त →   अक्शत   →   अक्षत

(क्ष is क + श)

The last letter to know has much to do with knowledge. It is said as 'Gna' or as 'Gnya' wherein the 'a's are अ.

ज्ञान	Gnan, Gnyan	(Knowledge)
आज्ञा	Aagna, Agnya	(an order)
द्राक्ष	Draksh	(Grapes)

☞   These two letters are in fact, conjoined consonants, and have evolved as special charatcters.

☞   Note that in pronouncing the conjoined consonants, the accent is on the letter that precedes both of them.

Punctuation Marks:

In addition to consonants and vowels, our writing contains punctuation marks. Fortunately at present, they are used exactly the same way in Devanagari, as they are in English. The same comma (,), quotes (' ') or (" "), question mark (?), exclamation mark (!), and so on, are used, not to leave out the semi colon (;), and colon (:).

☞ In modern Sanskrit, punctuation marks are used the same way as in English, except the period.

The comma and the quotes are not used in classical Sanskrit. Modernized Sanskrit writings do contain all the modern punctuation marks. There is some slight difference though. The period (.) at the end of a sentence, is represented in Devanagari as a vertical line, without any horizontal line at the top, thus: l.

This is a boy.   This is a boy l

His name is Ashok.   His name is Ashok l

Sometimes you may see two such lines, especially in a stanza of a poem.

टवीन्कल टवीन्कल लिटल स्टार
हाउ आई वन्डर वोट यु आर   l
अप अेबोव ध वर्ल्ड सो हाय
लाइक अ डायमन्ड इन ध स्काय ll

Were you able to read the above, word by word?

→ It is "Twinkle, twinkle, little star!"

Numerals, Fractions, and Decimals:

Words are made of one (a, I) or more letters of the alphabet. Numbers are made of one (1-0) or more numerals. Numerals are used in the same way as in English.

१	२	३	४	५
1	2	3	4	5

६	७	८	९	०
6	7	8	9	0

As you can see, the numeral 0 is identical, and 1, 2, and 3 are similar in both languages. The rest are easy to learn. Also remember, there is no horizontal line at the top of any numeral, or of punctuation marks.

☞ The numerals are used in the same way as in English. There is no horizontal line at the top of any numeral or of punctuation marks.

☞ All numbers, fractions and decimals are written the same way as in English. Mathematical symbols like plus (+), minus (-), times (x), division (÷), and square root (√) are used in the same way as in English.

२	x	४		=	८
१५	+	२०		=	३५
		१५²		=	२२५
		√२२५		=	१५

You have just completed learning all the consonants, vowels, punctuation marks, and mathematical symbols. Believe it or not, but now you should be able to read and write anything and everything written in the Devanagari script. Such statement can never be made for English. My most sincere compliments to you !

More About the Alphabet
A Review and Practice

This chapter should be sheer fun, provided you have been following the program instructions properly. If not, it may be a waste of time to go ahead. By now you should be able to read and write almost anything and everything that is written in the Devanagari script.

In the beginning of the previous chapter I threw the alphabet at you. Now I will show you slowly, how various letters are written. Also, I will help by showing you how to pronounce the sounds conveyed by certain letters properly.

I will give you a few hints to quickly recognize various characters, and will tell you many interesting tidbits.

In this chapter you will get more practice, making you feel more at home with the Devanagari script, and soon you will be prepared to take a real plunge in the Sanskrit language itself.

Write the numeral that is common between English and Devanagari.

→ ° (Zero)

Let us take another one. Take the letter "R", then split it in the middle vertically, I + २. The part on your right, "२" is Devanagari numeral २ (two).

Write the numeral two, in Devanagari.

→ २

The same numeral २, with a line at the top becomes the Devanagari equivalent of the letter "R", thus:

→ र

Write two Devanagari numerals, and one letter:

→ ०, २, र

What is the difference between the numeral two, and the letter "R" in Devanagari?

→ The letter has a line at the top, while the numeral does not.

२ (two), र (R).

The letter र is not called (AR) as in P<u>ar</u>k, but is called "r" as in Fu<u>r</u>. No ef (F), or ech (H), but simply "F" as in blu<u>ff</u>, or "H" as in <u>H</u>ut.

☞ Devanagari letters are named after the sounds they convey.

☞ In Devanagari, "0" (Zero) does not double as the letter "O" (Operator).

Which Devanagari numeral doubles as a letter?

→ २

Which letter does it become?

→ र

What sound does that letter convey?

→ R

Can you write "twenty" in Devanagari?

→ २० (Not र०)

Two hundred?

→ २०० (Not र००)

You should not be surprised that 2, 20, 200, etc. are written in the same way in both languages. Why not ?

→ The zero was invented in India for this purpose. Then it went to the Western world.

Let us take another letter. You do recognize the "S" as in Sam, Sleep, etc. We can put it to sleep, and cut it in the middle with a vertical line, like this: क. Note the line at the top. This letter is equivalent of "K", or of "C" as in Cut, Doc, Lock, etc.

How do you pronounce क ?

→ "K" sound as in Kite, Cut, Doc

It does look like two "C"s with a cut in the middle, doesn't it?

With a slight modification of क, we get another letter, which is फ. It is pronounced as "PH" or "F". There is no distinction between these two sounds in Devanagari.

How would you say फ ?

→ "F" as in Cuff, or fur.

This letter फ does remind me of an "F" which has fallen over on its back, to our left.

Write in Devanagari:

Cuff	→	कफ
Rough	→	रफ
Fur	→	फर
Of	→	ओफ.

० (zero) does not double as a letter. "ओफ" is incorrect.

34

Read:

कर	→	K.R
रक	→	R.K
o	→	Zero. It is called "Shoonya". You do not have to remember that.

We did look at the letter "S". In Devanagari, there is a letter which is written in the same way, like this: ड. This conveys the "D" sound, as in Dog, Doll, etc. When you write "d", you may wonder whether it is written as "d" or as "b". The letter ड is for a dilemma, and it apparently combines parts of "d" and "b" to remind us how to write it! Although it may look different in print, it is written like the letter "S", thus: ड.

Write in Devanagari:

Duck	→	डक
Two Duck(s)	→	२ डक
No Duck	→	o डक

The letter ड with a dot in the upper notch, like this: ङ is another letter, one with a nasal sound, like "ong/ung" as in Tongue. This is an interesting letter, in that no word begins with it. In the modern descendants of Sanskrit, ङ is never actually written. In Sanskrit it is written, but it is often replaced with a dot on top of the previous letter.

35

Say these:

ड	→	D
ङ	→	Ung/Ong
Dunk	→	डंक
Fund	→	फंड
(Ge)rund	→	(Ge)रंड

In Fund and Gerund, the dot represents "N", whereas in "Dunk", it represents ङ. Say "Dunk" and "Fund" out loud a couple of times to see the difference in the nasal sounds.

Which English letters convey the nasal sounds?

→　M and N.

These also occur in Sanskrit. Later, I will show you how to write these. So, there are N and M, plus there is ङ, that makes three. There are two more, for a total of five letters with nasal sounds.
Don't let that bother you. All five, each one, when used to represent a nasal twang, can be represented by the dot on the top of the previous letter. Of the five, only *M* and *N* may occur at the beginning of a word, while ङ and the other two nasal letters do not.

Use English letters (Devanagari ones, if you know them) and the dot to write the following:

Pump	→	ṖP	पंप
Bunk	→	Ḃक	बंक
Bump	→	ḂP	बंप
Bunt	→	ḂT	बंट

Write "Tongue" (as before)   →   ंग   टंग

You can easily write Pump using Devanagari letters also. You write "P" backwards, like this: "q", and then open it up, and put a line at the top, as always: प. This is "P" as in P<u>u</u>mp .

Write:

Pump	→	पंप
Punk (mud)	→	पंक
Kump (a shiver)	→	कंप
Puff	→	पफ्फ

Note how similar प (P) and फ (Ph) are.

Couple	→	कपल
Dump	→	डंप

The letter प can be modified to make a numeral: ५, which resembles a calligraphic lower case "y". This is the numeral 5. Its relation to the letter प is a bit more obvious in Devanagari, wherein the numeral ५ (5) is called "Punch" as in Hawaiian Punch. "Punch" means "Five".

Write:

Punch	→	पंच
Three Devanagari numerals	→	०, २, ५
Write Six Devanagari letters	→	र प क फ ड ङ

By now you really understand the concept of representing the nasal sounds with a symbol (■) rather than a whole letter. In English, you have to

37

write Pump, Tongue, etc, while in Devanagari a mere dot (■˙) will do, where ■ is any letter of the alphabet.

There are twelve such symbols to simplify our life. The dot is only one of them. Most of the remaining symbols stand for vowels.

Write English vowels: →   A, E, I, O, U.
Write a few combinations of these vowels to
produce different sounds.   →   AU,   EE,   OO, etc.
Write the symbols for these.   →   ■ी, ■ी, ■ॢ·

Writing The Devanagari Letters:

In English, all capital letters neatly fit between two horizontal lines: ADGTBNHJMOVCXS.

The lower case letters may fit between the two lines, or they may project above and/or below the lines: acsxz bdkl pquj.

Some do this only part way: **ABCD tji.**

However, all the letters can be accomodated in three equal segments, created by drawing four lines:

ABCD mncszx tfji pqbdy. Abq_n

In the above, **mncszx** occupy the middle segment. Let us compare this with Devanagari.

As you know, there are no capital and lower case letters in Devanagari. However, we have various vowel symbols that extend above and below the main letters. However, the proportion of various letters allotted to these spaces is slightly different.

The projections above and below the lines are only half the height of the main letters. That is, if we divide the writing space in four equal parts (not three), then the main body of the letter occupies the middle two parts, leaving one part above, and one below. Note the proportions:

क प र जा ला मि शी डे टै यु सू ई

You may want to use a blank sheet of musical scores to write Devanagari letters. Parts of a few letters themselves also extend above and/or below the lines:

क ख   ह क्ष भ ञ झ

In the above, the first two letters are confined to their own space. The remaining ones extend either in front of the top line, e.g., क्ष, भ

or below the base line, e.g., ह, क्ष, ञ, झ, or

both, e.g., क्ष.

Similar But Not the Same:

As you can see from the table of Devanagari and English letters, there are several groups of similar letters. See त, न, म, and भ.

As you know, न and म are nasal. You may also remember that they can be represented by a dot over the previous letter, as in the following:

पंकज

डंक

सेइंट   (a saint)

सेंट   (a scent)

One clarification is in order. They are not always replaced by dot. For example:

मनीषा

निखिल

अमेरिका

मेडीसीन

In these, म and न are used as such, with a vowel attached to them. It is only when we need the half or incomplete (without a vowel) म or न sound, that is, when we need ᠇ or ᠆, then and only then we can replace them with a dot.

The न sound is similar to "N", and is quite familiar to you. It is a dental sound. You can hold your tongue between your teeth and say it. This is the location as well, when you say थ as in थीम (theme).

Now say "Tom", then keep saying "T". Now, try to say न from the same location as ट. Or while saying न..न..न..न..न repeatedly, keep sliding the tongue upward and backward. When the न sound changes, let it change, and repeat that a few times. That is ण, another nasal character, used just like म and न. ण is used very commonly. However no word begins with it.

The last nasal letter conveys the "yn" sound, and it is written as ञ. No word begins with that either.

List the letters with which no word begins: → ण, ञ, ङ, ळ

Which of these letters are practically never written at all?

→ ञ, ङ

What sounds do they represent?

→ "yn", and "ung"

Let us write a few words with the ण sound:

माणेक	A precious stone
पारसमणी	A mythical stone, which converts everything it touches, into gold. "Midas" stone.
पाणी	Water
पाणिनी	The first one to formally write the grammar of Sanskrit.

Today there are many who would rather die than bother to study Sanskrit grammar. It is said that the great grammarian Panini actually gave up his life for it.

Once, while he was engrossed in teaching the Sanskrit grammar to his disciples on the bank of a river, suddenly a tiger appeared there. Disciples screamed, व्याघ्रः ! व्याघ्रः ! ("Tiger! Tiger!"). Panini simply gave them the etymology of the word saying, विशिष्ठा जिघ्रा यस्य सः व्याघ्रः । ("One who has a keen sense of smell, is called a Tiger"!) Disciples, less interested in the grammar, ran away. Tiger did what tigers do. Such was Panini's devotion.

41

Write:

Chakrap<u>a</u>ni   →   चक्रपाणी (ऋ=क + र)

(one who has a wheel in his hand. Lord Vishnu)

Padmini   →   पद्मिनी (द + म)

Patang   →   पतंग A kite, a moth

Conservation of Energy and Resources:

Let us go back to the word राम. The way it is written in English, RAMA, it can be pronounced in several ways.

Write in Devanagari, how RAMA can be pronounced:

→   राम,   रामा

रमा   रम

If we pronounce "A" as in Pat, a boy, man, etc. then there are many more ways it can be written.

In Devanagari, it can be said in only one way, राम.

Now you may appreciate, why it is a waste of time and energy to transliterate Sanskrit into English.

What is "Transliteration"?   →   To write something from one language in the script of another one. For example:

राम RAMA.

How does it differ from translation?   →   Translation gives the precise meaning using words and script from the new language.

Give some examples of translation and transliteration from this book or from elsewhere:

पंक → Punk (Transliteration).
→ Mud (Translation).
मन → Mana (Transliteration),
→ Mind (Translation)

Sanskrit and its daughters are phonetic languages, i.e., you read exactly the way it is written. Pronunciation does not have to be guessed. English words like Busy, Wonder, Lieutenant, etc. would be impossible for an outsider to pronounce correctly the first time.

Therefore, it is far more reasonable and efficient for one to learn the Devanagari alphabet than expect the entire Sanskrit literature to be transliterated into English. There are many advantages of learning the Devanagari alphabet.

I will not ask you to enumerate the advantages of learning the Devanagari script. One obvious advantage is, you may claim your position as an in-sider, rather than remaining a stranger.

By now, you have a basic concept of how the Devanagari script works, and how it differs from English.

Which one or more of the following would you consider as being helpful to you?

❑ Sanskrit is a phonetic language. So you read it exactly as it is written.
❑ Instead of writing out entire vowels, you write only their symbols.

❑ Sanskrit being a member of the Indo-European family of languages, it shares some words and characteristics with English.
❑ Sanskrit numerals are used in the same way as the English (Arabic) ones are.

Add any more advantages that you can think of:

→ 1.
2.
3.
4.
5.

Together or Apart?

In this chapter, we will go over some important and peculiar points of the Devanagari letters. It is easy to confuse RV (रव) and KH (ख). You can tell them apart by looking at the closeness of र and व in ख. The top line may have a small gap between र and व, in रव. When you know the words, the context may help differentiate them.

☞ Do not confuse the following similar looking characters:

रव	र व
ख	KH
श्व	श + व,
स्त्र	स + त्र (व or त + र)
स्र	स + र

Bite Your Tongue!

Another trouble spot for Westerners is in the following letters. In English, both rows are written as follows:

T   Th   D   Dh   N

ट   ठ   ड   ढ   ण
त   थ   द   ध   न

Each row of Devanagari letters above belongs to a distinct class. Its member letters are pronounced while the tongue is touching the same part of the mouth. The lowest row sounds are dental. You can literally hold the tongue between your teeth and say these letters. We did that when we talked about न.

You probably have no trouble saying न as in Nut, थ as in Theme, and ध as in There. Now, try to say the त and द while holding your tongue between your teeth.

The same is the case with the upper Devanagari row. For saying ठ, ढ, and ण, Try to say थ, ध, and न respectively, but without letting your tongue anywhere near your teeth. Say these by retroflexing the tongue, that is curling it up, and touching the palate with its tip.

All this is supposed to be fun. It may not make you laugh, but it should be of interest. I am not asking you to memorize anything. There is one quirk that deserves to be mentioned.

In the top Devanagari row, ठ and ढ both start out (in writing) as ट. Then, in ठ you have a complete loop, while in ढ there is a spiral, ending in a small loop.

Now for some genuine fun. ढ is the 14th letter of the alphabet. In my mother tongue Gujarati, a daughter of Sanskrit, there is a put-down for a stupid person or a moron, which goes like this: "(s)he is like a ढ", or "is the 14th letter of the alphabet!"

Why blame the poor ढ? Because the language has undergone profound changes from the parent languages of Sanskrit (Brahmi, etc.), through its daughter languages like Gujarati. While all other letters have been transformed severely, only ढ has managed to remain totally unaffected! I think it deserves to be honored.

Practice, Practice, Practice!

Your ballpoint pen is probably drying out. Try to write the following words entirely in the Devanagari script:

Car	→	कार
Food	→	फ़ूड
Done	→	डन
Mud	→	मड
Uncle	→	अंकल, अन्कल
Asia	→	एशिया
Austria	→	ओस्ट्रिया

Consulate	→	कोन्स्युलेट
Abort	→	एबोर्ट, अेबोर्ट
Hospital	→	होस्पिटल

One Less Sign to Worry About:

I hope you will forgive my regional pride, if I say that Sanskrit is much older than English, and therefore, it has no symbols to accomodate the broad "O" and broad "A" sounds as in *Hop* rather than *Hope*, or as in *(G)lad* rather than *Led.* The modern descendants like Gujarati, use a flipped sign for this: ◼. I had to use Gujarati fonts to show you this.

Dead	ડૅડ
Dad	ડૅડ
Fed	ફૅડ
Fad	ફૅડ
Hope	હૉપ
Hop	હૉપ

This sign is not used in Sanskrit, because before today no one has had the temerity to write English words in the script meant for Sanskrit!

***

It is never adequate to show you in writing how to pronounce a particular sound. Sometimes we have no choice. But you do have a choice. Probably there are people around you, among your family, friends, etc. who can show you the correct pronunciation, once and for all. I am just trying to help you follow what they might say.

An audio or a video tape is not the answer. Learning the mother tongue, or the mother of mother tongues is a family affair, and there should be no wedge to separate one from the family. Unlike in German, or in French, one does not have to learn how to pronounce each and every one of innumerable words. In case of Devanagari, you have to know the pronunciation only once.

The More the Merrier!

When we looked at the letters for Bh, Ph, Gh sounds, we did not talk about the Ch sound. Of course you are familiar with Chair, Child, Chore, etc. However, there is a minor difference. The two parts of Ch, that is, "C" and "h" are not related to each other.

There is no real "C" sound, unlike the "B" or "P" sound. Yes, there are two sounds conveyed by "C", viz., "K" sound, as in Cat, Cut, Catch, etc., and the "S" sound, as in Nice, Cycle, Choice, etc., but no "C" sound as such. Therefore, "CH" by itself is a unique sound.

What's the point of this whole story? Well, like Bh, and Dh, we also have a CHh sound. Again, you say the CH and H together, as in "Ah..ch.hoo!" or in "Ch.hu...ch.hu" train. The letter for that is छ.

See: लांछन   A blemish

छत्र   A head shield

छत्री, छाता   An umbrella (in Hindi)

Aspiring to Learn:

As your list of equivalents will show you, there are many letters in Devanagari, that stand for two letters in English, e.g. ध, फ, घ, ख, भ, etc., which stand for Dh, Ph, Gh, Kh, and Bh respectively.

Westerners have no problem with the first five, but the last one throws them off. In these letters, "h" is pronounced simultaneously with the preceding letter, and not sequentially. We say "Philosophy", and not "Pahilosopahy".

Similarly, "Bh" is not pronounced as "Bah". As in the first four letters, combining "h" with another sound, produces an entirely new sound. The original two sounds are not discernible anymore.

Write the following words containing the letters with an "h" sound (called "Aspirates", because you have to breathe in before you can say them out loud):

Jazz   →   जाझ

Rough   →   रफ

Them   →   धेम

Ghost   →   घोस्ट

Paksh (wing, sides in a dispute)   →   पक्ष

Bharat   →   भरत

Bh<u>a</u>rat	→	भारत. India's official name, after a king called भरत.
Ayatolla Khoummani	→	आयातोल्ला खोमेनी
George Bush	→	ज्योर्ज बुश
Washington	→	वोशिंग्टन

The Third Half:

Just to review quickly the various ways to create conjoined consonants. As you may recall, all English letters are half, or devoid of a vowel. The Devanagari ones already have the vowel अ included in them. You also remember that some letters like त, न, म, ग, have a दंड or "a stick" built in them, while others like ट, ड, ठ, do not.

What are the ways you can get a conjoined consonant,

1. From a letter with a दंड? → Remove the दंड, and then join it to the next letter, लास्ट

2. If there is no दंड? → Literally join it to the next letter, एक्टर

You did remember these two ways of getting a half letter. You also know one more, although you may not remember it as such. Let me refresh your memory.

3. What about half म and न ? → Put a dot on the preceding letter. That's the third way, पंप, बंट

4. Can that also be done for any other letters? → Yes, with ञ, ण, ङ

5. Which letters are practically never written out? → ञ and ङ

There is yet another and easier way to obtain a half letter. This is not an extra burden, unless you are working hard to commit all this to memory. This is one more tool to help you. The best part is, it works with any kind of letter, be it nasal, with a दंड, or without one. Ready?

I am sure you still remember the "inverted check mark" ◢ sign that we put on top of a letter, मेरी (Mary, Marry, Merry). A similar sign at the bottom of any consonant ◣ will make that consonant half. Let us go back to Smita and Bhaskar.

How do we write these?

Smita → स्मिता

Bhaskar → भास्कर

Sent → सेंट

Sant (A saint. How similar!) → संत

Can you write "Sant" in three ways? → १. संत

२. सन्त

३. सन्त

51

Using the new way we just learned, write

Smita	→	स्मिता
Bhaskar	→	भास्कर
Sent	→	सेन्ट
Fantastic	→	फेन्टास्टीक

☞ Do not confuse ▬ with ▬ Look at these carefully:

भास्कर   भासूकर (a meaningless word)

Please note that while we treat conjoined consonants as one letter, the half letter obtained in the newly learnt manner is treated as an independent entity. Compare the following:

स्मिता   समिता

This ▬ way of making a half letter is used extremely commonly. You will see many many examples of it as we go along.

A Curse In Disguise !

Just one last item before we conclude. It won't be fair to leave you unattended in the forest of conjoined consonants, especially when any half letter is joined to र.

Let us get "RI" or ऋ out of the way. It is a vowel, and is used either as such, or as ▪ as in पार्ट, or as ▬ as in कृष्ण.

52

रु is same as रु
रू रू
ऋ RI, there is no ◼ी.

For reasons beyond the scope of the present work, when any half letter is joined to र, the र disappears, and a tent like sign is put at the bottom: ◪ of the supposedly half letter, which looks like anything but half !

Tram	ट्राम
Drama	ड्रामा

When the half letter has a दंड, only half the tent sign ◪ appears in the angle between the दंड and the main body of the letter:

Progress		प्रोग्रेस
Cross		क्रोस (क्रोस)
Kendra	(Center)	केंद्र, केन्द्र
Shriman	(Mr.)	श्रीमान्
		(श्रीमान्, श्रीमान्)

Thank you for your patience, although I have been doing all the work. We must enjoy the journey also, rather than asking every few minutes "Are we there yet?" We have been talking about vowels, their symbols, consonants - half and full, numerals, and punctuation marks, etc.

Now you are ready to meet formally, the Devanagari alphabet itself. There is nothing for you to do. Just sit back and enjoy.

53

ENGLISH EQUIVALENTS OF
DEVANAGARI VOWELS AND CONSONANTS

Consonants:

क	ख	ग	घ	ङ	(No word begins with ङ)
k	kh	g	gh	ng	

च	छ	ज	झ	ञ	(No word begins with ञ)
ch	chh	j	jh/z	yn	

ट	ठ	ड	ढ	ण	(No word begins with ण)
t	th	d	dh	n	

(As you know, the pronunciation of the letters in this row, and in the next one below this, are not identical)

त	थ	द	ध	न
t	th	d	th	n

प	फ	ब	भ	म
p	ph/f	b	bh	m

य	र	ल	व
y	r	l	v/w

श	ष	स	
s	sh	sh	(The middle one is used less frequently)

ह	ळ	(No word begins with ळ)
h	r/l	

क्ष	ज्ञ	
ksh	gnya	(Actually, these two are special conjoined consonants)

Vowels and Their Symbols:

अ	आ	अि	ई	उ	ऊ		ऋ		
∎	∎ा	ि∎	∎ी	∎ु	∎ू		∎ृ	◌	∎ृ
A	Aa	I	EE	U	OO		Ri	Part	Krishna

ए	ऐ	ओ	औ	अं	अः
∎े	∎ै	∎ो	∎ौ	∎ं	∎ः
E	Ai	O	Au	Um	Ah

Special Symbols:

∎	Indicates a half letter	सन्त, फ्लीन्ट
∎	As in Tram, Drama	ट्राम, ड्रामा
॒	As in Progress, Creation	प्रोग्रेस, क्रीएशन

Alphabetical Order:

Devanagari alphabet is read from left to right, and from top to bottom. It goes from क to ज्ञ. First of all, note that there are 12 vowels, and 36 consonants. Also note that,

क्ष   is   क्श, or कश

and   ज्ञ   is   ग्न or ग्न्य

Therefore, in a dictionary, क्ष will appear under क, and ज्ञ will appear under ग.

It is also important to note that the vowel ऋ follows ऊ, and precedes ए.

There are many Sanskrit into English dictionaries available. Now you should be able to take advantage of them.

The alphabetical order is this:

Vowels
Consonants

Arrange the following in alphabetical order:

बोम्बे   ➝ अमेरिका

अमेरिका   बोम्बे

लंडन   लंडन

Under each consonant, just like in any English dictionary, the words will be listed according to their second and subsequent letters.

Arrange the following in alphabetical order:

कार   ➝ कम्पाला (युगान्डा)

कोमेडीअन   काउ Vowel first

क्रोस   कार Then consonant

काउ   कोमेडीअन

कम्पाला (युगान्डा)   क्रोस Half letter last

Don't let the following bother you. You may never need this. Each letter will be listed in the order of its accompanying vowel. That is, क, का, कि, की, ...कौ ।

कं, कः are applied to each of these. So, the order will be क, कं, कः, through कौ, कौं, कौः. This will then be followed by the half letter: क्ट, क्प, क्र (क्र), etc., again in the alphabetical order of the complete letter.

Everything In Its Proper Place:

Below, I have grouped the first 25 consonants in a 5x5 box. There is a very impressive order in that arrangement.

Say each row (horizontal) out loud, one after the other, and note that all five letters in any row are pronounced by keeping the tongue and lips, etc. in one particular way.

Where are क....ङ said from? → The throat. All the way back. These are *Gutturals.*

च...ञ → From the soft palate, at the back of the roof of the mouth. These are *Palatals.*

ट...ण → From the hard palate, retroflexing the tongue.

त...न → These are *Dentals.* Your tongue has to touch the back of your teeth.

प...म → These are *Labials.* Note your lips getting into the action.

Now, if you still have difficulty in pronouncing a letter, you can try to pronounce it in the same way in which all the other letters from the same row are pronounced.

All this is very interesting. Mind you, we are dealing with a language that is 5-10,000 years old. What a scientific and orderly arrangement!

The extreme right hand column (vertical) shows all five nasal sounds, ङ, ञ, ण, न, म. Note that each group (row) has its own nasal sound.

Which of these nasal letters are written and used as whole letters?

→ न, म, ण.

When used as half letters, all five can be replaced or represented by a dot over the previous letter. The pronunciation of the dot is automatically governed by the letter that follows.

Once again, let me demonstrate this to you. I have given below a few words using a dot. The first letter is ब in all of them, while the letter after the dot is different. Read these out loud, and notice how the sound represented by the dot varies.

Bunk	बंक	बङ्क
Bunch	बंच	बञ्च
Bunt	बंट	बण्ट
Bundh	बंध	बन्ध
Bump	बंप	बम्प

In the above, the letter after the dot is in order, from the क, च, ट, त, प group respectively. You do not have to do anything in this.

☞   The pronunciation of the sound represented by the dot is *automatically* decided by the letter just after it. No conscious effort is required.

There is more to this order that will interest you. There are many things we do in

English without quite knowing why we do them. For example, look at the words *Education*, and *Punctual*.

Write in Devanagari:

Education   ➝ एज्युकेशन

Punctual   ➝ पंक्च्युअल

What has happened?   ➝ D has become J in एज्युकेशन and T has become CH in पंक्च्युअल. Please do not say ""Di", "Je", "Ti", and "Si-Ech". Just say the sounds.

Now, this is in English, not in Sanskrit. We don't even bother to think about such things in English. There is a good reason for this: It is all done automatically. We don't have to think about it.

☞   Remember that well. *We don't have to think about it. We don't have to memorize it.* Ignorance of this simple fact has compelled innumerable students of Sanskrit to engage in memorizing tens and hundreds of "rules" for such changes. Spare yourself the trouble.

Look at the Devanagari alphabet we just saw. Notice how close ड and ज are, and how close ट and च are.

Whenever two consonants are joined together, or when two vowels occur next to each other, some changes in pronunciation automatically take place. They are interesting to look at. We will cross that bridge when we come to it.

Cut That Out !

Before we leave the alphabet, let me show you one last symbol. It is actually a punctuation mark, which is used extremely commonly in Sanskrit.

It is like an apostrophe mark — a sign of deletion— e.g., Boy's, It's, You're, I'm, etc. It looks like the English letter "S".

Which Devanagari letter looks like "S"?

→ ड

So, how would we write this new symbol ?

→ Like this: ऽ

It is called अवग्रह चिह्न (ह + न). You don't have to remember that, but it is good to know the signs by their names.

What's the difference between ड and the new sign ऽ?

→ Punctuation marks do not have a line at the top.

ऽ is generally used to indicate a missing अ. For example:

कालः अपि
कालो अपि
कालोऽपि

We will see many examples of that later. For now, let me just show you how it compares with similar Devanagari letters:

ड ऽ इ

Note that it has no line at the top. Also compare it with ड quite well to see that it doesn't quite extend to the baseline, nor does it have a miniscule vertical line suspending it from the top.

How do we pronounce it? Well, we don't! It is a punctuation mark, not a vowel symbol. It is not a letter of the alphabet. Then why don't we cut it out? Because, if we do cut something out, we'll have to put that sign there. And that's why I had to show it to you !

✳✳✳✳✳✳✳✳✳✳✳✳✳✳✳✳✳✳✳✳✳✳✳✳✳✳✳✳✳✳✳

PART: II
THE FABRIC OF SANSKRIT

·· ·

Now, we are ready to use our knowledge of the Devanagari alphabet. Read the following:

यथा चित्तं तथा वाचा → यथा....तथा = As is .....
So is.
चित्तं = Mind,
Thinking
वाचा = Speech.
As is (their) thinking, so is their speech

यथा वाचा तथा क्रिया । → क्रिया = Action.
As is their speech, so is their action;

चित्ते वाचि क्रियायां च → In thinking, in speech, and in actions;
च = and. Note the double त (त्त) in चित्ते, as opposed to a single त.

महतां एकरूपता ॥   →   महतां = Of the Great
Ones.
एकरूपता Uniformity,
एक = One,
रूप = Form. रू = रू

The above four lines together constitute a
श्लोक or a stanza.

Do you understand what this श्लोक means ?

→ *The great ones say
(only) what they
mean, and they
practice what they
say. There is a con-
sistency of their
mind, speech and
action.*

Like it?   Read it again. If you really liked it,
you will recite it again and again, and before you
know, you will remember it!   You do not have to
though.

Such a श्लोक incorporating a good saying is
called सुभाषित (सु = good, भाषितं = is said). There
are many excellent सुभाषित in संस्कृत. Many have
been used as proverbs in modern Indian languages.

Note that, at the end of the 2nd and 4th lines
of the श्लोक above, we used one or two vertical
lines as punctuation marks. They indicate a half
and full stanza respectively.

A single vertical line is used as a period (.),
in संस्कृत "prose" or गद्य (you can read this, गद्य
correctly? It is a half द् plus य)   As opposed to

64

that पद्य is "poetry". A great deal of संस्कृत साहित्य (literature) is in पद्य, and that makes it easy and fun to recite and remember.

The words यथा, तथा, and च are always used unchanged. Such words are easier to learn. They form important links in any language. You have to learn them once and for all. Then use them again and again.

Such words are called अव्यय ("no change"). You may want to keep a separate list of them. They are our real friends.

☞ अव्यय are the words that do not change, regardless of the gender, number, or case. They are a great help in building the vocabulary quickly and painlessly.

What do यथा, तथा, and च mean?

→	यथा =	As is...
	तथा =	So is
	च =	And

Such is not the case with all other words. Look at वाचा and वाचि.

What is their meaning?	→	वाचा =	"Speech"
		वाचि =	"In speech"

What is चित्तं ?	→	Mind, thinking
चित्ते	→	In the mind
क्रिया	→	Action
क्रियायां	→	In action<u>s</u>

65

Can you write क्रियायां in another way? → क्रियायाम्

You do remember "Cases" in English or in Latin. Maybe, you have forgotten all about them, intentionally perhaps! I don't blame you. Cases indicate the relationship between a noun and an action.

Someone (Nominative case) may be doing something, or is the object of that action (Objective), action may be coming to, or going away from him/her, or (s)he may be addressed by someone else.

In Sanskrit, there are eight such cases to recognize, not to memorize. चित्तं, वाचा, and क्रिया are the subjects of our statements. They are in the Nominative case. They are being named as doers of this or that. That is the First Case in संस्कृत.

The forms चित्ते, वाचि, and क्रियायाम् indicate "in", that is, place, and are therefore in the "Ablative Case for Place". That is the Seventh Case.

You must have noted that क्रियायाम् means "in actions". This is plural, while चित्ते and वाचि are singular.

How do you say "One" in Sanskrit? → एक. Remember एकरूपता?

Do you remember वाचा? → Speech

So, can you guess what does एकवचन mean? → Singular. "Speaking of one"

If बहुवचन is plural, then what do you think the word बहु means?

→ Many

Write in Sanskrit:

Singular	→	एकवचन
Plural	→	बहुवचन

Great! Do not work hard to memorize this, but you cannot forget एक and बहु.

Can you write "And" in Sanskrit?   →   (Read on)

If you could, good. If not, I will give you a hint. It is a one-letter word. We already saw it.

Can you find it, and then write it?   →   च (चित्ते, वाचि, क्रियायाम् च)

As you may have observed, now we are not talking about "Devanagari" anymore, but are talking about Sanskrit. We are using the Devanagari alphabet characters, but we are into the language itself. We studied च as a character or letter of the alphabet. Now, we are looking at it as a word.

Write	Singular in संस्कृत.	→	एकवचन
	Plural	→	बहुवचन
	"singular and plural"	→	एकवचन च बहुवचन

(Read on)

Good, but it is not correct. You can write that in two other ways, both of which are acceptable:

एकवचन च बहुवचन च
एकवचन बहुवचन च

However, the way in which we wrote एकवचन च बहुवचन, is not the correct way to

67

write it. This is probably because in संस्कृत, each word carries its full address in a sentence. And the way we wrote above, doesn't quite make it clear, which other word is to be linked to it.

All this may look unfamiliar and different to you. That is understandable. However, संस्कृत is not as unfamiliar to you as you may believe. In English, and in and around your (Indian) family and friends, you may have read or heard, and even spoken, a few संस्कृत words.

There are many संस्कृत words that are used in English, at times with a slight change in their meaning. I mentioned a few words in the beginning of the previous section.

Can you recall any? → Candy

Even if you do not know their meanings, you may still know a few संस्कृत words used in English.

Write those words in English and in संस्कृत:
- → Maya माया (Illusion)
- → Yoga योग (Union. Excercises to achieve a body fit for union with God)
- → Nirvana निर्वाण (Salvation)
- → Mantra मंत्र (त्+र) (a chant)
- → Guru गुरु (a teacher)
- → Pundit पंडित (a scholar)

→ Brahmin ब्राह्मण
(ह् +म) (a teacher)

→ Satyagraha सत्याग्रह
(Passive Resistance)

→ Swastika स्वस्तिक (a
benevolent Aryan
symbol, misused by
Hitler)

→ Dharma धर्म (Religion,
duty)

→ Karma कर्म (Deeds)

In Yoga, Mantra, Swastika, Dharma, Karma, etc., the terminal "a" is not pronounced as "a", while in Maya, it is.

There are many Sanskrit words that you may have heard, which are not used in English, but are used every day in your family, if you are from an Indian family.

Try to recall a few:

→	पत्र	a letter
→	नमस्ते	Hello
→	मित्र	a friend
→	सिंह	a lion

Many of the names of people you know, are also Sanskrit.

Can you think of any?

→	दिनेश	the Sun
	दिन	a day
	ईश	master
→	मनीषा	Mind's desire
→	निखिल	Entire

→	उषा	Dawn
→	सुधा	Elixir
→	अरुण	The Sun's charioteer (a noun), color orange (an adjective)
→	शांति	Peace
→	आशा	Hope
→	विजय	Victory

There are many words in modern Indian languages, which are altered somewhat, but are derived from Sanskrit. For example:

सूरज	from	सूर्य	(the Sun)
हाथ		हस्त	(a hand)
हाथी		हस्ति	(an elephant)
वाघ		व्याघ्र	(a tiger. Remember, "the one with a keen sense of smell"?)
रात		रात्रि	(a night)

There are many more. You may want to try and collect some. That will give you a head start with building your vocabulary.

If you have been going to Indian temples, you may know a few more words:

List them:

→	भगवान	(Lord)
	पूजा	(Worship)
	प्रणाम	
	वंदन	(to bow)

70

Names of gods, God: →   ब्रह्मा
विष्णु
महेश, (शिव)

These three gods constitute the Hindu Trinity. ब्रह्मा is the god of creation, विष्णु is the one to look after the day to day operation of the universe, and महेश, (शिव) is the god of destruction as a prelude to re-creation.

    →   राम
लक्ष्मण
सीता

From the epic रामायण, Lord राम is an incarnation of विष्णु, सीता is the devoted wife of राम, who was kidnapped by the demon रावण. लक्ष्मण is one of the three brothers of राम.

Characters from the epics and scriptures: →   युधिष्ठिर
कर्ण
कृष्ण
नारद

Books: →   रामायण
महाभारत
वेद (The Vedas)

Rivers, mountains: →   गंगा (the Ganges)
यमुना
ब्रह्मपुत्रा
हिमालय
(the Himalayas)

Believe it or not, but all these names are Sanskrit. You may not realize, but names of many Hindi movies from "Bollywood" are also Sanskrit. For example:

सत्यं, शिवं, सुंदरम् ("Truth, Benevolence, Beauty". These are the three attributes of the Lord)

स्वामि (Husband)

आक्रोश (Anger)

उत्सव (Festival)

Ask around if possible, and collect five more such words:

→ १.

२.

३.

४.

५.

Before we proceed, let me tell you this. The study of Sanskrit can be made very difficult and tedious. On the other hand, it can also be made fun. We are trying to keep it fun.

We are not denying that there is much to be said for accuracy, purity, and for the complicated rules, declensions, and conjugations, and other grammatical details.

If you want to go into all these, and personally I do like all this, there are many scholarly works in English, and in other languages for that. What I am doing is to show you a sample of the inherent beauty of Sanskrit, and to get you interested in that superbly delightful language.

Let me give you an example of the possible torture, which you are entirely spared. "There are three genders, viz., masculine, feminine, and neuter. There are singular, dual, and plural numbers, and there are eight cases. There are nouns with various endings, each one changing with its gender, number, and case. There is no choice for you, but to memorize these, before we can go further !"

That is not my style or philosophy. We can manage without memorizing any of the above, and still have lots and lots of fun along the way. We would rather remember सुभाषित or सुभाषितानि in plural, and that also by and by.

* * * * * * * * * * *

Let us read another सुभाषित.

गंगा पापं, शशि तापं

→ पाप =   Sin

ताप =   Heat

शशि =   Moon

The holy river Ganga (Ganges) removes one's sins, the Moon removes the heat (with her cool rays).

दैन्यं कल्पतरुः तथा ।

→ दैन्यं =   Poverty

कल्पतरु   The wish-fulfilling tree from the heaven. It makes all wishes come true.

तरु =   a tree

तथा =   And.

"The कल्पतरु removes one's poverty".

Note another meaning of तथा = "and". You may remember यथा..तथा = "So is...As is".

पापं, तापं च दैन्यं च → "All three". See again,

च = "and".

घ्नन्ति संतो महाशयाः ॥ → घ्नन्ति

(they) destroy, remove

संतो = (saints)

महाशयाः

(of lofty attitude)

महा = Great

आशय =(with) purpose.

"Company of great people can remove all three woes".

There are three kinds of woes, viz., spiritual, physical, and worldly. There is a cure for each one of them. However, contact with a good person can cure all three at once.

Do you know how? → "By keeping you out of harms' way".
Think more about this.

What is the case of गंगा? → First. "Nominative, for subject".

And of शशि तथा संतो ? → The same, first.

What are पापं, तापं, दैन्यं, as opposed to "subject"?

→ Objects. They are in "Second Case for Objects".

74

What is the seventh case?

Ablative for place, time, "In". चित्ते वाचि क्रियायाम् च

How do you like that सुभाषित? A great deal has been said about "good people", not all of them being saints, or hermits. Most of them are actually quite ordinary people, like you and me.

Another सुभाषित says that "In as much as God cannot come to this world everyday to take care of his business, he sends good people here"! They are literally, God-sent.

While we are talking about God, let us look at a prayer. Mind you, I am not trying in the least to teach you or convert you to the Hindu religion or culture as such. However, संस्कृत is the language of both of these. So, while you learn संस्कृत, you get the other two for free.

Now please read:

कायेन वाचा मनसेन्द्रियैर्वा → मनसा इंद्रियैः वा

काया = Body

What is वाचा? → Speech. Remember यथा वाचा तथा क्रिया

What is मन ? → Mind

इंद्रिय = Sense organ

वा = Or

"By/with (my) body, speech, or mind"

बुद्ध्यात्मना वा प्रकृतेः प्रभावात् । → बुद्धि = Reason, a faculty of mind

आत्मा = Soul

प्रभावात् Stemming from the influence or प्रभाव

प्रकृतेः of my nature or प्रकृति

"By/with (my) reason or soul"

यद्यत्करोमि सकलं परस्मै → यत् यत् करोमि

यत् = What

यत् यत् or यद् यद् Whatever

करोमि = I do

सकलं = everything

परस्मै = to the Supreme

"Whatever I do, to the Supreme......"

नारायणाय एव समर्पयामि ॥ → नारायणाय

to Narayana (God)

एव = Only

समर्पयामि I offer, I dedicate.

Can you figure out the meaning of this prayer?

→ *"Whatever I do with my body, speech, mind, sense organs, or by my very nature, I dedicate all that to the Lord alone."*

In other words, He is the doer, I am only an agent. In this श्लोक, कायेन, वाचा, मनसा, इंद्रियैः indicate "by or with a tool, means, etc." that is the Third Case.

What is the	First Case?	→	Subject
	Second?	→	Object
	Third?	→	Means, tool
	Seventh?	→	Place, "in"
	Fourth?	→	I will tell you now.

नारायणाय means "to (for) नारायण". This is the Fourth case. It is for the recipient, or for whom something is being done (receipient, purpose).

The Fifth Case is truly "ablative", indicating separation, i.e., "stemming from". प्रभावात् means due to, or because of, or thanks to the influence प्रभाव.

Influence of what? Of प्रकृति or nature, or personality. That is anything one does automatically. By the influence of my nature. That is the Sixth or the Possessive Case.

Let us review all the cases, and their English equivalents:

First		→	Nominative. Subject
Second	To	→	Object
Third	By, with	→	Means
Fourth	For (to)	→	Purpose, receipient
Fifth	From	→	Ablative separation
Sixth	of, ■'s	→	Possessive
Seventh	In	→	Ablative place
Eighth	O Lord! Hey man!	→	Vocative address

In the last श्लोक, which word was in the sixth case?

→ प्रकृतेः

Which word was in the eighth case? → None. Read on.

The next श्लोक has many examples of the Vocative or the Eighth case. It invokes or addresses the Lord by His various names.

श्री कृष्ण ! गोविंद ! हरे ! मुरारे !
हे नाथ ! नारायण ! वासुदेव !

→ These are all names of Lord Krishna, or Lord Vishnu, whose 10th major incarnation or अवतार is Krishna.

श्री. is a respectful address. It is a short form of श्रीमान्. It means "Mr." when used for a man. श्रीमती is "Mrs." The root word is श्रीमत्. Although श्री is used for gods, holy books, holy institutions, etc., श्रीमती is not used with names of godesses.

Let me give you the original names, so that you can appreciate the changes they have undergone to be in the eighth case.

कृष्ण	No change
गोविंद	No change
नारायण	No change
वासुदेव	No change
हरे	From हरि
मुरारे	From मुरारि

For reasons I will tell you shortly, nouns take a different form according to the case. Let me illustrate this using the word राम that you are so familiar with.
I will list its forms (declensions), and you give the meaning:

१.	रामः	→	राम does something	
२.	रामम् (रामं)	→	To राम (Object)	
३.	रामेण	→	By राम	
४.	रामाय	→	For राम	
५.	रामात्	→	From राम	
६.	रामस्य	→	Of राम, राम's	
७.	रामे	→	In राम	
८.	हे राम !	→	O Ram!	

The words नाथ, नारायण, वासुदेव, गोविंद, कृष्ण are similar to राम, in that, they all end with an अ (र्+आ+म्+अ).

Try to write (OK to cheat) the declensions of नाथ.

→
नाथः	नाथम्
नाथेण	नाथाय
नाथात्	नाथस्य
नाथे	हे नाथ !

The same will apply to ज्होन, बोब, ज्योर्ज, etc.
Try to do that with माइकल:

→
माइकलः	माइकलम्
माइकलेन	माइकलाय

माइक्लात् माइक्लस्य
माइक्ले   हे माइक्ल!

हरि has इ (short "i") ending, ह्+अ+र्+इ. Its declensions are as follows:

हरिः	हरिम्
हरिणा	हरये
हरेः	हरेः
हरिम्	हे हरे !

Don't be overwhelmed with the differences. Look at the similarities. The first four cases are nearly identical, so is the eighth one. If you do not start to memorize, the other three cases are not difficult to identify.

मुरारि is मुर + अरि. That is, "enemy of the demon named मुर. अरि and मुरारि both have इ ending, and hence, they would have the same declensions as हरि.

मुरारिः	मुरारिम्
मुरारिणा	मुरारये
मुरारेः	मुरारेः
मुरारिम्	हे मुरारे !

You can continue to refer to what we have just studied, and answer the following.

What is the meaning of

नारायणस्य ?	→	Narayan's
नाथे	→	In Nath (= Master)
गोविंदम्	→	To Govind (object) "a cowherd". Compare with Christ, the shepherd.
(नमो) वासुदेवाय	→	(I bow) to वासुदेव
रामात्	→	From राम
हे भगवन् !	→	Oh भगवान (Lord) ! भगवान is a general word for God. From भगवत्

Just for your interest,

वासुदेव (कृष्ण) is son of वसुदेव. In English, you have a hard time deciding whether Vasudev is the son or the father!

जानकी (सीता) is the daughter of the king जनक.

वैदेही (सीता) is another name of Sita. जनक was the king of विदेह.

पार्वती is the daughter of पर्वत (meaning, "a mountain", that is हिमालय).

द्रौपदी is the daughter of king द्रुपद. द्रौपदी is the wife of the five brothers (पांडवाः), in the epic महाभारत.

वैदर्भी is another name of द्रौपदी, because she was from विदर्भ.

In the श्लोक beginning with कायेन वाचा, we came across a couple of verbs.

Can you list them?	→	करोमि, समर्पयामि
What does the -मि ending suggest?	→	First person singular.
What is the English pronoun for that?	→	"I", the capital "I", for myself. "I am doing..."

Do you re-call the meaning of करोमि, समर्पयामि?

→ "I do, I dedicate".

The Sanskrit word for "I" is अहम् or अहं. Let us put this knowledge to use:

अहं गच्छामि   I go, I am going.

अहं वदामि   I speak

अहं चरामि   I walk.

The root words are respectively,

गम् (गच्छ)   To go

वद्   To speak

चर्   To walk

There are a few interesting points that we should note. One, there are no capital letters in Sanskrit. Nor is the infinitive "To", as in To go, To walk, etc. Also, each word in itself carries enough information to enable us to place it properly in the context.

☞ There are no capital letters in Sanskrit.

☞ There is no infinitive, e.g., "to go".

☞ Each word in itself carries enough information to enable us to place it properly in the context.

In the above three sentences, even without the word अहं, we can easily come to the same conclusion about their meaning, by looking at चरामि or वदामि alone. चरामि means अहं चरामि.

Since each word tells us its full meaning, and its relation to other words, there is no need for a definite word order in a sentence. Change the word order in the following sentence:

A tiger eats a goat.
A goat eats a tiger !

This would not be a problem in Sanskrit. We know that here "goat' is an object (grammatically).

What case would that be?   →   Second

Assuming "Goat" to be a Sanskrit word, how would we write that in the Second Case?

→   गोटम्, गोटं

Do you recall the Sanskrit word for "A tiger"?

→   व्याघ्र

Can you write that in the form of a subject?

→   व्याघ्रः

What case is that?   →   First

One more point. There are no articles in Sanskrit either.

☞ There are no articles in Sanskrit.

Write three English articles: →   A, An, The

So, we write: व्याघ्रः eats गोटम् ।

Shuffle the words as much as you want. Still, the meaning of this sentence does not change. The subject and the object are always identified unmistakably. Therefore, you need not memorize the word order.

☞ You need not memorize the word order.

In English, the word order changes when, instead of making a simple statement, you want to ask a question.

> This is a book.
> Is this a book?

No such thing in Sanskrit. However, nothing comes for free. There is a price to pay. In order for each word to be identified properly, it has to carry an identity card of sort, and the nouns are modified according to their gender, plus number, plus case, plus their endings.

Similarly, verbs are modified according to their tense, plus the mood, plus the voice, plus the person, and also the number, among other things.

How can you memorize all this? → You can not.
So, what should we do? → Don't try to memorize anything at all.

We know so many people with different heights, weights, occupations, color of their eyes, etc. But when we meet a person, we recognize him/her without consciously thinking about their height, weight, etc. Only rarely do we say, "That looks like John, but I am not sure. He walks a bit too fast, and he looks too tall". The same is true for words. You do not recognize people from their phone numbers!

What is the word for "I"? → अहम्

The word for "You" is त्वम्. And for He, She, and It are सः, सा, and तत् respectively. These are the first case singular forms of the pronouns अस्मत्, युष्मत् and तत् respectively. You can forget these right away.

You may be able to see some similarities. सः is like रामः and indeed, is the masculine first case singular form of तत्.

सा is She. आ ending is feminine. So is the long "I" or "EE" ending ई (अी). You may know some Indian women or girls, or you may be familiar with names of some Indian godesses. Try to recall names with such endings.

Write five names each, with आ and ई endings.

→ आशा, मनीषा, अरुणा, उषा, वंदना.

→ कामिनी, सौदामिनी, गौरी, गुणवंती, सुंदरी.

Names of godesses? → सरस्वती, लक्ष्मी, पार्वती, सीता

Write English names with these endings: → Marla, Donna, Lisa. Sandy, Juli, Dolley.

Write all personal pronouns in Sanskrit:

→ अहम्   I

त्वम्   You

सः   He

सा   She

तत्   I t

तत् is not much different than "That".

Write the verb-ending for the pronoun "I":

→ -मि

Write:

I go.   → अहं गच्छामि।

I walk.   → अहं चरामि।

Do you recognize the vertical line at the end?

→ Yes. That's the sign for a period (.).

Now we are using the sign for the period, because now we are writing full sentences.

What about the verb-endings for I, You and for He/She/It?

-मि   I

-सि   You

-ति   He/She/It

-मि is of course for Me. -सि is for "Si, senior!" (Yes, Sir!) for You.

Note that -मि, and -सि are used regardless of gender, and -ति is also used for all three, He/She/It. There is a reason for it. This is not a major exercise in grammar; it is common sense.

Nouns are affected by the gender. Pronouns are noun substitutes. So they are also affected by gender. Adjectives modify nouns and pronouns. So, they also are affected by gender.

☞ Verbs and adverbs are not affected by the gender.

Write:

I go	→	अहं गच्छामि।
You go	→	त्वं गच्छसि।
He goes.	→	सः गच्छति।
She goes.	→	सा गच्छति।
It goes.	→	तत् गच्छति।
She walks	→	सा चरति।

Can you write that in another way? → चरति सा।

Write:

I speak	→	वदामि अहम्।
You speak	→	वदसि त्वम्।
It goes.	→	तत् गच्छति।

Note that in addition to the endings, there are some internal changes:

वदामि
वदसि
वदति

What do you see?	→	वदामि
	→	वदसि, not वदासि
	→	वदति the same.

You are not expected to know the meaning, but can you guess what is going on in the following sentence?

सर्पः दसति ।

→ Somebody or some-thing called सर्प (first case सर्पः for subject), is doing something (third person) दसति. Well, it says, *"The snake bites"*.

What is the Sanskrit word for Snake?

→ सर्प, not सर्पः, it can be सर्पः, सर्पेण, सर्पस्य

The word for

To bite? → दस्

To walk? → चर्

To go? → गम् (गच्छ्)

Most root verbs end in a half letter, like स्, र्, or च्.

You must be wondering about गम्(गच्छ्). Why is गम् there? Well, गम् is the root word. But the form गच्छ् is used in the present tense. गम् is used at other times, as a noun "going" (a gerund, or verbal noun, if you may). We say गमन (the act of going, departure), and आगमन or "arrival".

There is another word दृश् (पश्य्) Drish (Pashya), meaning, "to see". You can refer back and attempt to write the following in Sanskrit:

I see → अहं पश्यामि।

I see a tiger. → अहं व्याघ्रं पश्यामि।
व्याघ्रं अहं पश्यामि।
पश्यामि व्याघ्रं अहम्।
पश्यामि अहं व्याघ्रम्।

Although, at present you may believe that व्याघ्रं अहं पश्यामि। means "A tiger sees me", that is not so. अहम् is first person singular, and it is in the first or subjective case. व्याघ्रम् is the second or objective case form of व्याघ्र.

अहम् or अहं means capital "I", and hence, there is a Sanskrit word अहं, which is a noun, meaning "Pride" in a derogatory sense. It is a vice rather than a virtue. "He is full of अहम्" means "He is full of vanity or arrogance". So,

The noun अहम् is ....? → Vanity, pride
The pronoun अहम् is ....? → I, myself.

Much of the Sanskrit religious literature is about controlling and conquering the अहम् or the pride, and surrendering it into the greatness of God, i.e., merging the आत्मा (self, soul) into the Great परम, Soul आत्मा.

परमात्मा (परम + आत्मा= परमात्मा).

Can you separate the followings into the first, second, or the third person?

वेदसि	→	Second (You)
अस्मि	→	First (I)
मुह्यसि (ह् + य)	→	Second
जागर्ति	→	Third (He/She/It)
पश्यामि	→	First
करोति	→	Third
वेत्ति	→	Third

Did you make it? Great! If not, I will give you a hint. As you recall, -मि is the first person, -सि the second, and -ति is the third person. अस्मि, वेत्ति, जागर्ति are only apparently difficult, not in reality.

Would you like to know what these words mean? I will only tell you, if you promise me not to memorize them. When we use these words, you will remember them without any trouble. You may recognize at least one of them.

वेदसि	→	"You know".
		वद् = to know.
		वेदाः or the Vedas are the most ancient books of knowledge.
अस्मि	→	"I am".
		अस् = to be
मुह्यसि	→	"You are confused".
		मुह् = to confuse.

जागर्ति   →   "He/she/it stays awake"

जागृ =   to wake up.

पश्यामि   →   "I see". You did know this one, correct?

करोति   →   "He/She/It does".

कृ =   to do

कर्म = a deed, Karma

वेत्ति   →   "He/She/It knows".

Again, from वेद्

Even without realizing, you have just overcome a very big hurdle. You may have been impressed with the fact that वेत्ति did look different, and maybe जागर्ति (Jagarti) also. In fact, अस्मि and मुह्यसि are quite different as well, at least as compared to चरामि, गच्छामि, and वदामि that we knew so well.

What you did overcome is this. The verbs undergo a little change before -मि, -सि, or -ति is added to them. The change maybe either nothing at all, or adding अ, य, अय, etc. before applying -मि, and so on. Just look at the following:

वद् plus आ plus मि is वदामि

अस्   nothing   मि   अस्मि

मुह्   य   सि   मुह्यसि

वेद्   nothing   ति   वेद् + ति

वेत्ति = वेत्ति

जागृ   nothing   ति   जागर्ति.

Depending upon the changes they undergo before taking -मि, etc. the verbs can be divided into ten groups, called गण. The important point is again, that not knowing their गण did not prevent you from recognizing the sense of the above words!

In this language Sanskrit, where nouns (pronouns, adjectives) and verbs keep on changing all the time, there are words, believe it or not, which do not change, no matter what! We did come across a few such words.

Can you recall them? → यथा, तथा, च, एव, वा, हे!

What is their meaning?

यथा → So is

तथा → 'As is", "and".

च → And

एव → Only

वा → Or

हे! → Hey! O!

I mentioned nouns, pronouns, and verbs above. They are called "Parts of Speech" in English.

How many Parts of Speech are there? → Eight

Name the ones I did not mention. → Adverb, Prepositions, Conjunctions, and Interjections.

Can you sort out the following into their respective parts of speech?

यथा	→	Adverb
तथा	→	Adverb, conjunction
च	→	Conjunction
एव	→	Adverb
वा	→	Conjunction
हे!	→	Interjection

To refresh your memory, let us review what various **Parts of Speech** do:

1.	Nouns	→	Name an object, person, or feeling
2.	Pronouns	→	Substitute for nouns
3.	Adjectives	→	Qualify nouns, and pronouns, by stating their color, number, shape, size, etc.
4.	Verbs	→	Indicate the action
5.	Adverbs	→	Qualify action, e.g., how, where, when, why, etc.
6.	Prepositions	→	Indicate the relation-ship of two nouns, e.g., above, to, from.
7.	Conjunctions	→	Join two nouns, phrases, or parts of a sentence, e.g., "and, or, but, so".
8.	Interjections	→	Exclamatory sounds, e.g., O! Oh! Ouch! Hey!

You did not see any prepositions. Not because there aren't any in Sanskrit. Indeed there are several. You did use "to, from, for, with, in" etc. earlier.

Do you remember, in what context?   →   Cases. To Ram, by Ram, for Ram, In Ram

In English, we do not modify nouns according to their cases. Instead, we use these prepositions. That is why in English, we talk about only a few cases, viz., Nominative, Objective, Possessive, Vocative, and so on, and group the rest (with prepositions) under what is called "ablative" of time, or place, or means, etc. In Sanskrit, these are distinct cases.

Cases indicate the relation between a noun and an action. Prepositions indicate relationship between two nouns. We sorted यथा, तथा, च, एव, वा, हे! into prepositions, conjunctions, and interjections. But, we do know something else about these words, viz., they do not change.

What do we call non-changing words?   →   अव्यय

☞   Therefore, we can surmise that all prepositions, conjunctions, and interjections are अव्यय.

* * * * * * * * * * * *

94

Let us take another श्लोक :

आकाशात् पतितं तोयं
यथा गच्छति सागरम् ।
सर्व देव नमस्कारः
केशवं प्रति गच्छति ॥

You should be able to recognize the intent (not the meaning) of the underlined words. You tell me what you can, and I will tell you their meaning.

यथा	→	As is, As
गच्छति	→	He/She/It goes
प्रति	→	Towards
सागरम्	→	To सागर (sea), second case
केशवं	→	To केशव
आकाशात्	→	From आकाश (5th)
पतितं	→	Fallen
तोयम्	→	Water
सर्व	→	All
देव	→	Demigod, god
नमस्कार	→	Bowing down with hands folded together
Can you make sense out of this श्लोक ?	→	*Just as all water that has fallen from the sky, (ultimately) goes into the ocean, worshipping any other god(s) eventually goes to the Lord Krishna!*

In case you are wondering, all सुभाषित are श्लोक, but not the other way around. "Subhashitas" and "Shlokas" are not good ways to indicate their plurals. Their plurals are सुभाषितानि and श्लोकाः ।

'Singular" and "plural" are called "numbers". You do know what singular and plural are, and you do remember their Sanskrit equivalents, एकवचन and बहुवचन.

	→ I didn't expect you to remember that. If you did, great!
What does एक mean?	→ One
And बहु ?	→ many

There are many occasions, when we use the words "We" or "You" (plural), or "They", when more often than not, we are referring to only two people, a couple of friends, a husband-wife, or a boyfriend-girlfriend pair. Therefore, in Sanskrit, we also have द्विवचन. द्वि (Dwi) means two. So we have एकवचन, द्विवचन, and बहुवचन, or Singular, Dual, and Plural numbers.

You may correctly think that this is not really necessary. Today, all the languages of the world (correct me if I am wrong) are happily managing without the Dual form or the द्विवचन. However, we are not here to design a language, but rather to study it, and enjoy it. You will appreciate its beauty, once you see it used. You can always be thankful that you don't have to live with its quirks everyday!

Let us take the word सिंह (a lion) for example. Its first case declensions will be सिंहः, सिंहौ, सिंहाः and this means "a lion, two lions, and many lions".

Write the same for:

राम	→	रामः, रामौ, रामाः
व्याघ्र	→	व्याघ्रः, व्याघ्रौ व्याघ्राः
लक्ष्मण	→	लक्ष्मणः, लक्ष्मणौ, लक्ष्मणाः

What is हस्तौ ? → Two hands.

हस्त = Hand

You may not remember हस्त, but you should be able to say, "हस्तौ means two हस्त, whatever that may be".

What is कर्णाः ? → Many कर्ण, that is, many ears.

It may seem nonsense to talk about "many ears", when all of us have only two each, and it may make still less sense to talk about two or more राम.

There is some purpose behind all this. When we speak about राम and his brother लक्ष्मण together, we say रामलक्ष्मणौ, which you know is द्विवचन. The same is for the plural or बहुवचन. We can talk about राम, लक्ष्मण, and their two remaining brothers.

By the way, do you know their names? → भरत, and शत्रुघ्न.

शत्रु = "an enemy"

घ्न = "who kills"

पापं तापं च दैन्यं च
घ्नन्ति संतो महाशयाः

    While talking about all four brothers together, we say रामलक्ष्मणभरतशत्रुघ्नाः । Note शत्रुघ्नाः rather than शत्रुघ्नः। The latter is the singular form, while we need the plural one. I hope you did not have any trouble with त्र which is त् + र = त्र = त्र.

    Also note that I used the Sanskrit sign for the period after the four brothers' names. If I used the English one, it would have looked like the Braille writing. Look: शत्रुघ्नाः.

    You may also note that I combined all four names into one single word without any hyphen, rather than like this:

राम-लक्ष्मण-भरत-शत्रुघ्नाः ।

☞   Piling up words on one another,
without a hyphen is very common, and
is a characteristic of Sanskrit.

    Sanskrit words appear to be very long, and intimidating. You can easily break a word down into its various components, provided you possess at least some basic vocabulary skills. If not, you will come up with some interesting absurdity like:

रा मलक्ष्म णभर तशत्रु घ्नाः !

Now see this:

जगतः पितरौ वंदे → जगतः = <u>of</u> the
universe
पितरौ (two) parents
पितृ = a parent
वंदे = I bow to

पार्वतीपरमेश्वरौ → पार्वती Lord Shiva's
wife, "daughter of
mountain" (पर्वत),
that is, हिमालय.
परमेश्वर Lord Shiva.
"the great god"
पार्वतीपरमेश्वरौ (two)

These two lines are written by the great
कालिदास. He says:

*"I bow down to Parvati and Lord
Shiva, the parents of the universe!"*

You must have noted the similarity between
the root word पितृ and the Latin word "Pater" for
Father. "But", you will say, "in this, I am bowing to
them. So I am the subject, while they (पार्वती and
शंकर or शिव) are the objects". So, why do we still
say, पितरौ? Good thinking, and you are absolutely
correct. It is in the Second Case Dual form, which
is the same as the First Case Dual form.

In the second case dual form also the -औ
ending occurs:

99

First   ईश्वरः   ईश्वरौ   ईश्वराः
Second   ईश्वरम्   ईश्वरौ   ईश्वरान्

Recall राम:

रामः   रामौ   रामाः
रामम्   रामौ   रामान्

Can you guess why I selected ईश्वर, while talking about पार्वती and शिव (शंकर)?

→ Because शिव is the परमेश्वर,

परम = supreme

ईश्वर = God

We have seen several times by now, that when we link two words together, many interesting things happen:

परम + ईश्वर = परमेश्वर
अ   इ or ई   ए (ऐ)

सूर्य   उदय   सूर्योदय   → Sun + Rise = Sunrise
अ   उ   ओ

सूर्य   अस्त   सूर्यास्त   → Sun + Set = Sunset
अ   अ   आ

Two short sounds combine to make a long sound, as we can easily imagine. We shall see many more examples as we go along, but note that, in addition,

अ + अ = आ,
(Short) (Short) (Long)

उ उ ऊ, and

इ इ ई.

As always, no need to remember these phonetic changes, because they occur automatically, regardless of the language you are using. The grammarian did not make the rule, he just observed what people like you and I were doing.

After   Hour   "Afteravar"

आफ्टर   अवर   आफ्टरावर

Such unions are called संधि, meaning "a joint" or "a union". From that we get the word संध्या, which is "twilight' (union of two lights), and it includes उषा (Dawn) and संध्या (Dusk). Both these words are also used as names of girls. Many Sanskrit proper nouns are also parts of day to day vocabulary.

Now, let us write the declensions (forms) of राम in all cases and all numbers. Not that there is any religious reason for choosing राम, but traditionally, it is used as the type example.

राम (नर जाति) *RAM (Male Gender)*

Case	*Singular*	*Dual*	*Plural*
१.	रामः	रामौ	रामाः
२.	रामम्	रामौ	रामान्
३.	रामेण	रामाभ्याम्	रामैः
४.	रामाय	रामाभ्याम्	रामेभ्यः
५.	रामात्	रामाभ्याम्	रामेभ्यः
६.	रामस्य	रामयोः	रामानाम्
७.	रामे	रामयोः	रामेषु
८.	हे राम !	हे रामौ !	हे रामाः !

First of all, you don't have to commit this to your memory. I have divided the eight cases in unequal groups. In each group, there are one or more forms that are identical or similar. Also, the widely separated first and eighth cases are nearly identical. I want you to notice the similarities.

We used to memorize such tables (you have seen only one so far), and a few of us hated doing that. There were a few daredevils, like the present writer, who actually enjoyed that. Any young mind can easily commit this table to memory.

Chanting this table — it has nothing to do with Lord Rama's name — has its own rhythm and there is an inherent calming cadence. You may try to say the entire table out loud a couple of times. Do not say the case numbers out loud.

राम is a masculine noun, with an -अ ending. There are other nouns (not to forget pronouns, and adjectives) with two more genders, many more endings, viz., आ, इ, ई, उ, ऋ, and also with consonant-endings like त्.

In addition to these declensions, there are conjugations of verbs, with their ten groups, three numbers, three persons, and at least three tenses, and a few moods. All this can be enough to put you in a tense mood, but I will spare you all that.

The saving grace is that all these are more similar than different. Let us not forget that Sanskrit was spoken by people first, then the rules came. We can still learn the people's way.

Let us take another noun with an -अ ending. Such nouns are called अकारांत or "ending-in-an अ-sound". अंत means "an end" (अकार + अंत = अकारांत). Our next example is वन (a forest), which is an अकारांत noun like राम, but is in the neuter gender.

Name three genders: →   Masculine, Feminine Neuter (not "neutral")

In English, we use Masculine and Feminine genders for men and women according to their sex. The neuter gender is used for all animals and things. We do use "She" or "Baby" for our favorite cars, and marvel at the space shuttle lifting off, saying, "Ain't *she* magnificent!" The Moon, and our country are also "She".

In Sanskrit, the grammatical gender has very little to do with sex. Yes, men and women will generally fall into masculine and feminine genders, most of the time. However, there is one word for "wife" that is in the neuter gender, and oh yes! There is another one that is in masculine gender!

Well, what can I say? We don't discriminate on the basis of sex!

Back to the वन. Let me give you the declensions for the first two cases:

वनम्	वने	वनानि
वनम्	वने	वनानि

As our luck would have it, the forms for both cases are identical. Let me add that the eighth case is almost identical to the first two. Therefore,

१.	वनम्	वने	वनानि
२.	वनम्	वने	वनानि
८.	वन	वने	वनानि

To put the icing on the cake, even the rest of the cases are same as for राम (masculine).

Look up the declensions of राम above, and write those for वन.

१.	वनम्	वने	वनानि
२.	वनम्	वने	वनानि
३.	वनेन	वनाभ्याम्	वनैः
४.	वनाय	वनाभ्याम्	वनेभ्यः
५.	वनात्	वनाभ्याम्	वनेभ्यः
६.	वनस्य	वनयोः	वनानाम्
७.	वने	वनयोः	वनेषु
८.	वन	वने	वनानि

After a while, you will know right away, that -स्य is "Of", -षु is the plural form of "in", -भ्याम् is in the middle column, i.e., Dual, three times, and so on, and so forth.

Now is the time for one more सुभाषित. भाष् is the root word, meaning "to speak". Remember not to separate B and H, while saying भ. The word भाषा means "a language", and भाषण is "a lecture" or "a speech". What you are learning now, is संस्कृत भाषा. It is also called गीर्वाण भाषा, meaning "the language of the gods'.

What is the Sanskrit script called?	→	देवनागरी लिपि
what is लिपि ?	→	A script

★ ✳✳✳✳✳✳✳✳✳✳✳✳✳ ★ ✳✳✳✳✳✳✳✳✳✳✳✳✳ ★

Read the following:

विद्या विवादाय धनं मदाय
शक्तिः परेषां परपीडनाय ।
खलस्य साधोः विपरीतमेतद्
ज्ञानाय दानाय च रक्षणाय ॥

Do you know what the one (I) or two (II)
vertical lines above indicate?

→ The middle and the end of a stanza.

Do you know any of the above words? → च = And

What does रामाय mean? → For राम

What declension is that? → Fourth Case, singular

Find other words like रामाय. → विवादाय, मदाय, परपीडनाय, ज्ञानाय, दानाय, रक्षणाय

What are they trying to say (forget the meaning)?

→ For this or that.

Do you remember the meaning of रामस्य ? → Of राम

Any other similar words ? → खलस्य

What does it indicate? → Of खल

Let me tell you that खल means "a bad guy, or a cheat". As opposed to that, साधु means "a good person, or a monk". Let me tell you that this सुभाषित contrasts the behavior and character of खल and that of साधु.

Can you find the equivalent word for खलस्य? → साधोः

106

While we are at it (the third line), let me tell you that विपरीतम् means "opposite, to the contrary", and एतद् means "this" referring to the behavior.

What is the meaning of the third line,
खलस्य साधोः विपरीतं एतद् ?

→ "The behavior of good guys is opposite to that of the bad guys."

Now, we learn three "power" words.

विद्या	Education, learning
धन	Wealth
शक्ति	Strength

If you give these to the good guy, and to a bad guy, they will be put to strikingly different uses by each of them. Let me draw a table, contrasting the purpose (for) which each will use these three:

साधु *Good Guy*		खल	*Bad Guy*
ज्ञान	Knowledge	विवाद	Arguments
दान	Charity	मद	Arrogance
रक्षण	Protection	पीडन	Torture
		पर	Others

The point is, you cannot tell a good guy from a bad one by looking at whether (s)he has विद्या, धन, or शक्ति, since either of them can have these. It is the use for which these are applied, that

107

distinguishes the two. So, the sense of this श्लोक
is:

> Education is for arguments,
> wealth is for arrogance,
> And their strength is for
> harassing others
> in case of the bad guys; quite the
> contrary is for the good guys,
> they are for knowledge, donations,
> and for protection.

Note that all the words listed above ज्ञान,
दान, etc. are similar to राम and their declensions
are the same as those of राम.

Since we are contrasting the behavior of खल
and साधु, it is reasonable to guess that साधोः
carries the same sense as खलस्य, i.e., it is in the
Sixth or the Possessive Case Singular. That is
indeed so.

Which two words were in the sixth case singular?

→ खलस्य, साधोः

What is the basic word in खलस्य? → खल (अ-कारांत)

साधोः → साधु (उ-कारांत)

Ignoring the difference between singular and
plural, now we know three ways to express the
possessive case.

Can you list them? → खलस्य, साधोः, इषाम्

What does पर mean? → पर = Other(s).

Write the Sankrit words for:

Learning	→	विद्या
Wealth	→	धन (धनम्) is neuter, first case, singular.

Do you recall a similar word? → वन (a forest). Its declensions are similar to the masculine राम.

Except in the following cases:

१.	रामः	रामौ	रामाः	→	वनं वने वनानि
२.	रामं	रामौ	रामान्	→	वनं वने वनानि
८.	राम!	रामौ!	रामाः!	→	वन वने वनानि

Write the Sanskrit words for:

Arrogance, pride	→	मद
A good person, a monk	→	साधु
A bad guy	→	खल
Opposite	→	विपरीतम्

* * * * * * * * * * * * * * * * * *

While we are talking about the good guys, let me tell you, that's the kind of friends you want to have. Good friends are those who stand behind you in needs, and adversities. What are they like?

उत्सवे व्यसने चैव
दुर्भिक्षे शत्रुविग्रहे ।
राजद्वारे स्मशाने च
यः तिष्ठति सः बांधवः ॥

You do remember सः, सा and तत्. They are personal pronouns.

What is the meaning of	सः ?	→	He
	सा	→	She
	तत्	→	I t
Can you guess, what यः is ?		→	(One) who
What can you say about तिष्ठति ?		→	He/She/It does.....

स्था(तिष्ठ) = To stand

बांधव means "a brother, or a friend".

What is बांधवः ?   →   Like रामः, first case, singular

The fourth line says: "One who stands (with, or behind us) is (the real) friend".

Now, recall or look up रामे. What is it?   →   In राम. Seventh case.

Find similar words in this सुभाषित.   →   All words, except चैव, च, and the entire fourth line.

That means, we are talking about "in" all of those things. I have listed them below:

उत्सव	Festival, happiness
व्यसन	Hardship
दुर्भिक्ष	Famine
शत्रु	Enemy
विग्रह	Battle
राजा	King
द्वार	Door

राजद्वार	The king's court →	Note राज- not राजा here. We<u>ll</u> + Come = We<u>l</u>come	
स्मशान	Crematorium, a desolate place		

What does च mean? → And

→ चैव is च + एव.

एव is a filler word meaning "Thus". It enhances the meaning. चैव means, "and this too".

What is the सुभाषित telling us? → *"In all times, good and bad, in famine, in battles, in a king's court, and even in a graveyard, the one who stands with us is a real friend".*

In चैव,	च + एव = →	चैव	
	अ ए →	ऐ	
What is	अ अ →	आ	
		सूर्य + अस्त = सूर्यास्त	
	उ उ →	ऊ	
	इ इ →	ई (Short+short = long)	
	अ उ →	ओ	
		सूर्य+उदय = सूर्योदय	
	अ इ/ई →	ए. परमेश्वर	
Note:	च इव →	चेव	
	च एव →	चैव	

In this सुभाषित, there were a few instances in which two words were joined together.

Can you go back and find them?   →   शत्रुविग्रह
राजद्वार
चैव

In शत्रुविग्रह, the words शत्रु and विग्रह remain unchanged and easily identifiable. In राजद्वार, राजा becomes राज-, as we saw in "welcome", while in चैव, two vowels join and undergo a change. Interesting, isn't it!

Are you ready for some more fun? I didn't tell you, but I am sure you know this:

उ + अ → व.

Language is langvage.

इ अ → य.

Pity + able = "Pityable"

अ इ → ए (see above), and

अ उ → ओ

A + U = Auto (Oto)

I will say this again and again. You just observe the phonetic fireworks. This should not be a burden to you.

Why not?   →   Because it happens automatically.

* * * * * * * * * * * * * * * * * * * *

This time, I will tell you the meaning of the next सुभाषित first. It says:

> It is by effort alone, that the work reaches fruition, and not by fantasizing,
>
> No animal enters the gaping mouth of a sleeping lion (voluntarily. That is, he has to go and hunt for that).

Now the सुभाषित itself:

उद्यमेन हि सिध्यन्ति
कार्याणि न मनोरथैः ।
न हि सुप्तस्य सिंहस्य
प्रविशन्ति मुखे मृगाः ॥

In Sanskrit, adjectives take the same form as the noun they modify. So, "of a sleeping lion" would become "of sleeping, of a lion".

Can you find the two words that mean "of sleeping, of a lion"?

→ सुप्तस्य सिंहस्य

Which word is most likely to mean "in" the mouth?

→ मुखे (like रामे)

Animals → मृगाः

What is प्रविशन्ति likely to be?

→ They .... (enter)

Which word indicates the negative "no, not," etc.?

न. Good guess! That wasn't difficult, was it?

Those who study languages of the whole world tell us that in all known languages, the negative word invariably contains the N or न sound. For "Yes" it is not so.

हि is a filler to add emphasis. न हि means "of course not". हि in the first line also means "only, this is the only way".

The word उद्यम means effort or industry. What is
उद्यमेन हि?

→ "Only with effort"
Third case (tools)

कार्य is "activity, work, project". It is derived from the root verb कृ meaning "to do". कार्याणि is the plural form for the first, second, and the eighth cases:

कार्य	कार्ये	कार्याणि
वनं	वने	वनानि

Do not worry about न and ण. You should know how to pronounce them, but under certain phonetic conditions, they can replace each other automatically. There are rules describing their behavior, but you do not need to know them.

Can you guess the meaning of सिध्यन्ति?

→ They, these acts (succeed)

Therefore, कार्याणी उद्यमेन हि सिध्यन्ति ।

→ Projects succeed only with effort.

There is only one more word left: मनोरथैः ।
What does that mean?

→ "by fantasies", of course! This is plural,

third case, while उद्यमेन is singular.

रामेण, रामाभ्याम्, रामैः ।

मनोरथ contains two words, viz., मन and रथ.

What is मन ? → Mind

रथ is a chariot. मनोरथ means fantasy ("chariots of mind" literally). You can ride the chariots of the mind and reach anywhere in a nano-second, but if you don't get off your buttocks, you won't get anywhere. मनोरथ is a nice word. I hope you liked it. Sanskrit is full of such expressions.

* * * * * * * * * * * * * * * * * *

We talked about good guys, then about good friends, and about importance of action over fantasies. Let us look at the bad guys a bit more thoroughly. You cannot be too careful with them. They are worse than a snake. Do you know why we say that?

→ *The snake bites you only at times, while the bad guy bites you at every step!*

सर्पदुर्जनयोर्मध्ये → दुर्जनयोः + मध्ये

मध्य = Middle

मध्ये = Between

वरं सर्पो न दुर्जनः । → सर्प = a snake

दुर्जन = a bad guy

दुः = bad, or difficult.

Remember the word for Famine? → दुर्भिक्ष. That is "when it is *difficult* to get any food or alms by begging (by monks)".

→ जन = a person

वरं = better

"Of the snake and a bad guy, the snake is better, not the bad guy".

Word order is important here, because सर्पः and दुर्जनः both are in the same first case singular form.

सर्पो दसति कालेन

→ दसति = (it) bites

→ कालेन = "by time', at times, (third case, by convention)

दुर्जनस्तु पदे पदे ॥

→ पद = foot, step

पदे पदे = at every step (7th case, time)

दुर्जनः + तु = दुर्जनस्तु

तु = but

Note: सर्पदुर्जनयोर्मध्ये → सर्पदुर्जनयोः मध्ये

दुर्जनस्तु → दुर्जनः तु

दुर्जन → दुः + जन

The last of the twelve signs forming the बाराखडी, is ∎ः, and it is known as विसर्ग । When two words are joined, the विसर्ग can become a half र (Part पार्ट) as in योः + मध्ये = योर्मध्ये. or as in दुर्जन.

116

It may become a half स् as in दुर्जनः + तु = दुर्जनस्तु. Learn to recognize this change. It will help you in breaking down the complex words correctly into their components. Other examples:

नमः +	ते	=	नमस्ते	→ (I) bow to you!
गुरुः	ब्रह्मा		गुरुर्ब्रह्मा	→ Gururbrahma, say it correctly.
गुरुः	विष्णुः		गुरुर्विष्णुः	
विष्णुः	गुरुः		विष्णुर्गुरुः	
गुरुः	देवः		गुरुर्देवः	
देवः	महेश्वरः		देवो महेश्वरः	

→ देवो is देवः, सर्पो is सर्पः

This is not as difficult as it may seem. Look at one step at a time. All steps are basically the same. The whole line is:

गुरुर्ब्रह्मा गुरुर्विष्णु-
र्गुरुर्देवो महेश्वरः ।

→ Gururvishnurgururdevo

महा + ईश्वरः = महेश्वरः

List all the forms a विसर्ग can take during a संधि.

→ Half र, योर्मध्ये
Half स् दुर्जनस्तु
ओ as in सर्पो दसति

After the first two transformations, the two words were actually joined. In the third transformation, the विसर्ग was converted into ओ, but then the words were left separate.

Now we take a श्लोक from the famous Hindu holy book भगवद्गीता ("Lord-Sung", literally), about how even a good person can be destroyed and become a bad one.

→ भगवट् गीता

Try to separate out (विग्रह) the components of the underlined words:

ध्यायतः <u>विषयान्पुंसः</u>

→ विषयान् पुंसः

This is easy. Half न is joined to पुं.

<u>संगस्तेषू</u>पजायते ।

→ संगः तेषु

विसर्ग becomes half स.

तेषु उपजायते

Two short उ make a long ऊ.

<u>संगात्संजायते</u> कामः
कामात्<u>क्रोधोऽभिजायते</u> ॥

→ संगात् संजायते

→ कामात् क्रोधः

क्रोधः अभिजायते

This leads to,
क्रोधो अभिजायते
विसर्ग becomes ओ.
क्रोधोऽभिजायते

अ from अभि is dropped to avoid joining ओ with अ.

What changes can a विसर्ग undergo? → 1. (It may be dropped).

2. Become half स

3. Become ∎ ͨ

4. Become ओ.

     In the last संधि, or union, अ from अभिजायते is dropped, and that is indicated by the sign of deletion: ऽ, called अवग्रह (no need to remember this).

What is the word for a "sign" ? → चिह्न (half ह + न)

How does अवग्रह चिह्न differ from ड ? → The sign has
1. no horizontal line at the top,
2. nor does it have a small vertical up-stroke, leading up to the horizontal line,
3. It does not reach the baseline.

Why doesn't it have the top horizontal line?

→ Because it is a punctuation mark.

What else does not have the top line? → Numerals.

You don't have to know this, but do you recall what the two dots in पुंसः are called?

→ विसर्ग

This I haven't told you yet. Do you know the Sanskrit term for the dot on the top of पुं ?

→ अनुस्वार.

अनु- = follows

स्वर = a vowel

स्वार =

(makes an adjective).

Just for interest, it is called अनुस्वार, because it is pronounced after the vowel, that is, in पुं, we say प, then उ, and then finally, we say ∎. Again, just for interest, the five nasal letters are called अनुनासिक, because they "follow (the path through) नासिका the nose".

What does the above श्लोक tell us? It is about a (any) person, who keeps on thinking about pleasures for his sense organs like eyes, ears, etc. विषय means the domain of the sense organs.

विषय has several meanings. The commonest is a "subject". The विषय of the book you are reading now, is संस्कृत. In spiritual writings it means desires, especially the sexual ones. This is the saga of one who keeps on thinking about various विषयाः ।

Find the two words meaning "of thinking of a man":

→ ध्यायतः पुंसः

What other ways do you know to indicate the possessive case? Give three examples:

→ खलस्य, साधोः, -णाम् (plural)

Now, see the words उपजायते, संजायते, and अभिजायते. All these words share a common part. Can you find it?

→ -जायते

You may remember गच्छति, वदति, etc. What does -ति indicate?

→ Third person singular. He/She/It does something.

-ते has the same significance as -ति. So, -जायते refers to "He/She/It does something". The root word for जायते is very interesting. It is जन् (जा), meaning "to produce".

You should be able to recall the Latin root word "Genere" (to produce). It is used in words like Hydrogen (water producer), Oxygen (acid producer), Nitrogen ("Nothing" producer, inert). Also, it is seen in Genesis, Genus, etc.

Sanskrit root word जन् (जा) is also very commonly used. जननी (mother), जाया (wife, "one who produces"), सरोज (lotus flower, "born in a lake"), पंकज (also Lotus, "born in mud"), and so on.

उप-, सं-, अभि- are the prefixes (Pre = before). The Sanskrit word for that is पूर्वग (पूर्व = before). You do know गम् (गच्छ) = to go. So, it is something that "goes before".

However, when such prefixes are applied to verbs, and are made integral parts of them, they are known as उपसर्ग. They serve the same purpose as पूर्वग.

What is पूर्वज ? → "Born before", i.e., An ancestor.

अनुज → "Born after" A descendent.

अनुजा → A daughter.

121

उपसर्गाः alter the meaning of the verbs they are attached to. These are very useful and friendly words, like अव्यय. We will see many more later. For now,

उप-   Sub-   Under, following

उपनगर   Suburb   →   नगर   = a city

                                                          देवनागरी =

                                                          (the script) of the cities of gods.

सं, सम्   Con-   Together

संवाद   Conversation

अभि-   Ad-   Towards

अभिरुचि Affinity

Note that in the above examples, the prefixes are not attached to verbs, but are attached to nouns, and are therefore पूर्वग.

Let us go over the meaning of this श्लोक, ignoring the fine points for now. It says,

"Contemplating one's desires leads one to an attachment or संगः in them (तेषु, seventh case plural). From that संगात् comes a wish कामः। From काम, कामात् (when the wish is not fulfilled), comes anger क्रोधः। "

Say you saw a beautiful luxury car in a TV advertisement. It is obviously beyond your means. So it stays on your mind, and you keep on seeing it on the road. Then you start actively looking for it. Your mind is always seeing it, and soon, your mind stops seeing anything else.

Now you begin to hate your menial job which was paying your mortgage, and start hating your loving wife, mother of your young kids, for not working.

Let us re-trace the steps literally:

Of the man, contemplating pleasures
an attachment in them is produced;
from attachment, a wish,
from the wish, anger.

What are संगात् and कामात् ?   →   Fifth case, ablative of separation, "From"

The above श्लोक is one of a couplet. Let us go to the second श्लोक, to understand its full meaning. The Fifth case still predominates. Try to do the विग्रह (separation) of words united by संधि ।

क्रोधाद्द्रवति संमोह   →   क्रोधात् (द्) भवति
संमोहात्स्मृतिविभ्रमः ।   →   संमोहात् स्मृतिविभ्रमः
स्मृतिभ्रंशात्बुद्धिनाशो   →   स्मृतिभ्रंशात् बुद्धिनाशः
बुद्धिनाशात्प्रणश्यति ॥   →   बुद्धिनाशात् प्रणयति

In the above, find the half letters joined to the ones with a र sound:

→ क्रोध   (क् + र)
स्मृति   (स्म् + ऋ)
विभ्रम   (विभ् + र)
प्रणश्यति   (प् + र)

What is त्र ?   →   त् + र, त्र, व्र, त्र
What is द्ध (बुद्धि) ?   →   द् + ध

What is म्र (भगवद्गीता ? → द् + ग

भगवत् गीता

भगवद् गीता

भगवद्गीता

What happens next is all down hill. Once you start falling, there is no stopping before hitting the bottom.

From anger, comes confusion	→	भवति = Happens भू (भव्) = To be. संमोह means "clouded thinking"
from confusion, disturbed memory	→	स्मृति = Memory. It includes "everything we know" विभ्रम = Disturbance भ्रम् = to spin, to have an illusion or delusion
From delusion, loss of reason	→	बुद्धि = Intelligence, faculty of reasoning, judgement
from reasoning-loss, *(s)he is destroyed.*	→	प्र+ नश्यति = is ruined नाश = Destruction.

Find all the verbs from the couplet: → जायते, भवति, नश्यति

If you selected ध्यायतः, you are not wrong, and not quite correct either. It is a word derived from ध्या meaning, "to contemplate, to meditate" ध्यायतः is a part noun, and part verb (that is, "participle").

Just for interest, without being burdened by it, the word ध्यायत् means "one who is contemplating", and ध्यायतः is its possessive case singular — *the contemplator's*. Do you see, how complicated the study of Sanskrit can be made?

List all उपसर्गाः ।   उप-, सम्-, अभि-, प्र-

प्र + नश्यति = प्रणश्यति. Note the change from न to ण. Yes, there are "rules" for this also. Just try to say प्रनश्यति a few times, with a relaxed, slurred speech, and you will start saying प्रणश्यति, even if you couldn't pronounce ण well at first.

The उपसर्ग प्र- is similar to "Pro-" (further) as in Progress, Proceed, etc. So, प्रणश्यति means, "is progressively destroyed more and more, until its completion".

भू (भव्) is a very important verb. It means, "To be". Yes, the famous, "To Be, or Not To Be, that is the question!" I don't have to tell you that "am, are, is, was, were" are its various forms or conjugations. The verb भव् means "to be, to become, to happen, to occur".

You may want to go back and read both the श्लोकौ (dual form) together several times. These are two of the best श्लोकाः from the भगवद्गीता । Any young man or woman would do himself or herself a great favor to read this small book. It is indeed a treasure cove of सुभाषितानि, it presents the Hindu philosophy in a nutshell, and is the nucleus of the epic महाभारत ।

125

I certainly hope you are enjoying your learning so far. Sanskrit does not easily lend itself to simplification. Nor is it possible to do justice to it in a mere few pages. The श्लोकाः that I have selected for you, provide excellent wisdom, and excellent examples of declensions of many nouns, for various cases. Memorizing these श्लोकाः is a very pleasant alternative to memorizing declensions and conjugations.

Sanskrit poets have cleverly used the declensions of nouns in all eight cases, and woven them into a stanza. Their poetic prowess provides us with good mnemonics (memory aids).

The following, श्लोकः weaves all (singular, masculine, अकारांत) declensions of वीर (short form of महावीर, महा + वीर = Great + victor, over oneself, that is). Lord महावीर, born 2600 years ago, was the latest founder of the religion Jainism.

वीरः सर्व सुरासुरेन्द्रमहितो	→ Veer is honored by all gods, and anti-gods,
वीरं बुधाः संश्रिताः	→ To Him the learned ones reach for shelter
वीरेणाभिहतः स्वकर्म निचयो	→ By Him are destroyed his accumulated sins
वीराय नित्यं नमः ।	→ For Him, our respects, always.
वीरात्तीर्थमिदं प्रवृत्तमतुलम्	→ From Him springs this unparallelled religion (Jainism)
वीरस्य घोरं तपो	→ His is the great

वीरे श्री धृति कीर्ति कांति निचयः → penance

In Him is the निचयः collection of wealth, fortitude, prestige, glory.

श्री वीर! भद्रं दिश ॥ → O revered Veer! Show us the Salvation!

Separate the followings:

सुरासुर → सुर + असुर
वीरेणाभिहतः → वीरेण + अभिहतः
वीरात्तीर्थमिदं → वीरात् + तीर्थमिदं
तीर्थमिदं → तीथम् + इदं
प्रवृत्तमतुलम् → प्रवृत्तम् + अतुलम्

सुर + असुर are the celestial good guys and the bad guys. These gods, or demigods सुराः are quite minor, and as in Greek mythology, they are hopelessly human. But they are harmless, and they support the holy activities of the mortals.

The prefix अ- is a negative prefix. असुर means non-सुर. असुराः are the agents of Satan (there is no such single entity in Indian mythology, but any powerful असुर can become a Satan). They are devilish, destructive, and trouble-makers.

Both of them, सुराः and असुराः are always fighting. Either side can appease God, however, the असुराः with their reason blinded with greed, lust for power, for immortality, and their arrogance usually end up squandering all their might, inflicting endless torture on the सुराः, and the rest

127

of world along the way. In short, सुरासुर means "the good and the evil".

Actually, the श्लोकः we just saw is only four lines long, not eight. But I had divided each line into two segments. Here is a similar श्लोकः about Lord राम ।

रामो राजमणि सदा विजयते	→	Lord Ram, like the king jewel, always prevails
रामं रमेशं भजे	→	To Him, to the Blissful Lord, I bow
रामेणाभिहता निशाचरचमूः	→	By him was decimated the demon (Ravan)'s army
रामाय तस्मै नमः ।	→	For (to) that Ram, are my respects
रामान्नास्ति परायणं परतरं	→	Nothing or nobody is a greater protector than (from) Him
रामस्य दासोस्म्यहम्	→	I am His servant
रामे चित्तलयः सदा भवतु मे	→	May my mind always rest in Him
भो राम ! मामुद्धर ॥	→	Hey Ram! extricate me (from all the worldly woes) !

Do the विग्रह of the following संधि ।

रमेशं

रम + ईशं
रमा + ईशं

अ, आ + ई = ए
परमेश्वरौ

निशाचरचमूः

निशा-चर-चमूः
The three words are
joined unchanged.

निशा   = Night

चर   = to walk

निशाचर = Demons,
"Active at night"

चमू   = An army

रामेणाभिहता	→	रामेण	+ अभिहता
रामान्नास्ति	→	रामात्	+ नास्ति
दासोऽस्म्यहम्	→	दासः	+ अस्म्यहम्
अस्म्यहम्	→	अस्मि	+ अहम्
		अस्म्य्	+ अहम्
		अस्म्यहम्	

इ or ई + अ = य

Note that here ि

disappears, and य्

appears instead.

मामुद्धर   →   माम्   + उद्धर

These two श्लोकाः were unrelated, but were
similar. These श्लोकाः are in a meter called
शार्दूलविक्रीडित (Shardool-vikreedit). You may
want to request someone to show you how to sing
these and other श्लोकाः that we enjoyed so far.

Personal Pronouns:

We came across many nouns, pronouns, and participles used as adjectives. All of these undergo declensions according to their number and cases.

☞ Unlike English, the Sanskrit pronouns do not have the Vocative, or the eighth case for address. There is no such usage as "Hey you !"

You may miss "Hey you!", but there is a word भोः !, which is like "Hear ye! Hear ye !"

Declensions of the pronouns अस्मत् (that is "I"), and युष्मत् (You), are same for both genders. However, as we saw, तत् (It) does take different forms, as exemplified by सः (He), सा (she), and तत् (It), in their first case singular forms.

There are other forms of अस्मत् like अहम् ("I"), माम् (to me, me), मया (by me), मम or मे (of mine, my), मयि (in me), etc. You may recognize some of them in the following:

रामे चित्तलयः सदा भवतु <u>मे</u>
भो राम ! <u>मामुद्धर</u> !

As for युष्मत्, or "You", the first case forms are, त्वम्, युवाम्, यूयम्। Do I have to point out the similarity between "You" and यूयम् ? Some of the other forms are तव (your), त्वया (by you), etc.

The personal pronoun तत् varies according to gender. Let me show you only the first case singular, dual, and plural forms:

Masculine:	सः	तौ	ते
Feminine:	सा	ते	ताः
Neuter:	तत्	ते	तानी

These were the personal pronouns, viz., I, You, He/She/It. There are other pronouns like यत् (which), एतद् (this), etc. Each of these have their own declensions. All are easy to recognize. We will deal with these later, as also with other endings of nouns. You do remember:

यद्यत्करोमि सकलं परस्मै → यद् यद् करोमि
Whatever I do,
(I dedicate) all that...

त and द are interchanged many times in English also. Pardon the bad example, but I have heard "pistoff" instead of "pissed off". Also, how did we get the "Sunkist" oranges? Well, they are "Sun-kissed" !

* * * * * * * * * * * * * * * * * *

The next श्लोकः is also from गीता. It deals with the very foundation of the Hindu philosophy, and its emphasis on cultivating a feeling of detachment, especially towards one's body. It is about the soul, which is considered distinct from the body, and hence immortal. This श्लोक illustrates many verbs.

131

नैनं छिन्द्न्ति शस्त्राणि   →   न + एनं = नैनं

(Not this)
Weapons do not penetrate this

नैनं दहति पावकः ।   →   पावक "Purifier", fire.

fire does not burn this

न चैनं क्लेद्यन्त्यापो   →   क्लेद्यन्ति आपः

चैनं = च + एनं

"and this".
"*and, water does not wet it*

न शोषयति मारुतः ॥   →   *Wind doesn't dry this.*

Let me give you the meanings of all the words used. First the nouns:

शस्त्राणि	Weapons
पावकः	Fire
आपः	Water
मारुतः	Wind

Now pronoun and adverb:

न	No, Not
एनं	(to) this

Finally, the verbs:

छिन्द्न्ति	(They) penetrate
दहति	(It) burns
क्लेद्यन्ति	(They) soak, wet
शोषयति	(It) dries

*"Weapoms do not penetrate this (soul),
Fire burns it not;
And this, water wets not,
(This) the wind does not dry".*

Also about the soul from another verse in
गीता :

न जायते प्रियते वा कदाचित् → वा = Or
कदाचित् = Ever
प्रियते = Dies.

What does जायते mean? → He/She/It takes birth
*"The soul does not
ever take birth, nor
does it ever die"*
That is, it is the body
that dies.

The verbs may take -ति or -ते endings. Some
verbs may take either ending. Just for your reading
practice, these three groups are known as
परस्मैपदी, आत्मनेपदी, and उभयपदी.

उभय means "either, ambi-" as in
Ambidextrous (equally skilled with both hands), or
amphibian (can live both, on land or in water, e.g., a
frog). You will have no difficulty recognizing them.

The same is the case for various verb groups.
Each of the three groups I mentioned above is
divided into ten classes, called गण, each with its
own characteristic inflections, etc.

Again, you won't have to worry about these.
To you it won't make any difference, whether it is

वदति, or अस्ति, or खादयति, or करोति, (the first, second, tenth, and the eighth गण परस्मैपदी respectively) as long as you can understand that they all indicate that He/She/It is doing something.

Adjectives:

As for the adjectives, there is no need to remind you that all numbers are adjectives too. There are simple adjectives like लघु (small), गुरु (large), रक्त (red, orange), etc.

A good many of the adjectives are created by literally joining several words. We saw an example of nouns joined together: रामलक्ष्मणभरतशत्रुघ्नाः । Just like nouns, many a time, whole descriptions and attributes are combined and used as adjectives.

In English, many such words are joined with hyphens:

A "quicker-picker-upper" paper towel.
"Don't-you-dare-tell-me-that" look.
"George Washington, a plantation-owner-from-Virginia, the Commander-in-Chief-of-the-Continental-Army, became the first President of the United-States-of-America"

Now, in the next section, we will look at many such adjectives, and many examples of the eighth case, Vocative for address. It is actually a prayer of Lord शिव or शंकर. You remember Him from जगतः पितरौ वंदे पार्वतीपरमेश्वरौ ।

नमो नमस्ते भगवन्   →   I bow, bow to You,
                          O Lord!

दीनानां शरणं प्रभो ।   →   Shelter-of-the-poor,
                          O Lord ! दीन = Poor
                          शरण = Shelter

नमस्ते ! करुणासिन्धो !   →   I bow to you.
                          O Ocean-of-mercy !
                          करुणा = Compassion
                          सिन्धो = Oh सिन्धु
                          (Ocean).

The northwestern part of the Indian subcontinent is blessed with many large rivers like गंगा (the holy river Ganges), यमुना, ब्रह्मपुत्रा (ह् + म) and सिन्धु. The last river is called सिन्धु, because it looks like a sea. Indian Aryan civilization flourished on the banks of सिन्धु and other rivers. From "Sindhu", we got "Indus" and "India', as well as "Hindu". संस्कृति is "Civilization", and संस्कृत means "Civilized".

नमस्ते मोक्षदायक ॥   →   I bow to You, O
                          Giver of Salvation
                          मोक्ष = Salvation
                          दा (यच्छ) = to give
                          दान = Donation.
                          Note the similarity.

करचरणकृतं   →   Committed by (my)
                    hands or feet.

कर = Hand, from

कृ = to do.

चरण = feet, from

चर् = to walk.

वाक्कायजं कर्मजं वा । → Born of (my) speech, body, or action.

जन् (जा) to be born,

वाक् = वाचा

काया= body,

कर्म = deed, action, from

कृ = to do.

वा = or

You probably have heard of the theory of कर्म (Karma) and पुनर्जन्म (re-birth).

श्रवणनयनजं वा → Born of hearing or seeing.

नयन = an eye

श्रवण = hearing,

शृ = to hear.

When the ancient knowledge collected in the four वेदाः or the Books of Knowledge, was lost, it was recreated *from memory* in the books called "Memories" or स्मृति (the Smritis), of these, मनुस्मृति compiled by मनु is quite well known.

136

When स्मृति books were also lost, they were re-written by *listening* to the older sages. These books became known as श्रुति (The Shruties). The next time around, the scholars *sat down next to* their गुरु (Gurus, teachers), and created उपनिषद् (the Upanishadas). उप- = Sub-, next to. नि + सद् = to sit down. I hope you are not memorizing this.

मानसं वापराधम् ॥	→	वा अपराधम् Or the lapses of mind. मानस = mind अपराध = fault, crime
विदितमविदितं वा	→	Known or unknown, knowingly or unknowingly विदितम् अविदितम् वा विद् = To know. वेदाः The books of knowledge.
सर्वमेतत्क्षमस्व ।	→	सर्वम् एतद् क्षमस्व Forgive all these सर्वम् = All एतद् = This क्षम् = to forgive क्षमस्व is a request or command. "You do this (please)".
जय जय करुणाब्धे !	→	Glory, Glory to You! O the Ocean of Mercy!

करुणा = Compassion, as we already saw it.

अब्धि = सिंधु

= an ocean

अब्धे ! = O ocean !

अब्धि = अब् + धि, that is "one that holds water". Recall "water does not soak this (soul)" or न चैनं क्लेदयन्त्यापो । अब् and अप् both mean "water".

श्री महादेव शंभो ॥ → Revered Great God शंभु !

महा = Great

देव = god

श्री is a respectful address, and salutation for people, gods, saints, and even things (श्री बाइबल).

शंभो = Vocative form (address) of शंभु, Lord शिव, or शंकर । शंभो, सिंधो, प्रभो are similar, from शंभु, सिंधु, प्रभु.

This prayer asks forgiveness from Lord Shiva, for various lapses and sins. In addition to शंभो, and प्रभो, there are many more ways in which the Lord is addressed, or referred to. Most of them describe the Lord, and are made of several words joined together.

Find such words, and tell me their meanings:

मोक्षदायक	→	O, the Salvation-giver
दीनानां शरणं प्रभो !	→	The poor's shelter, O Lord !
करुणासिंधो	→	O, the ocean of Mercy
करुणाब्धे	→	O, the ocean of Mercy
महादेव	→	O, The great God All these of course refer to Lord शंकर.

Since शिव is a masculine noun, almost all the above take a masculine form, and are in the eighth or the vocative case. Only the word दीनानां is in the possessive case, and शरणं is in the first or the nominative case, and is in the neuter gender. In the prayer, these words are followed by the vocative masculine address प्रभो.

सिंधु and अब्धि both mean "an ocean". The former has an -उ ending, and is called उकारांत. The latter has an -इ ending, and hence, is called इकारांत.

So far, we have seen the combined-words-adjectives for शिव or शंकर.

Can you find such words describing the lapses or अपराध, and say their meaning ?

→ करचरणकृतं
Literally, "hand-feet-done"

वाक्कायजं Speech-body-generated,

139

कर्मजं action-born,
श्रवणनयनजं hearing-
eye-generated,
विदितमविदितम्
Known-unknown.

The last line of the prayer, श्री महादेव शंभो
also appears in some versions as सच्चिदानंददेव !

सत्	means	Truth, or the Verity
चित्		Sensitivity, Life
आनंद		Bliss

The Lord is the Verity, the Life, and the Bliss.
That is the description of the Supreme Divine
Element or ब्रह्म.

सत् + चित् = सत्चित्
= सच्चित्
(Punctual)

चित् + आनंद = चितानंद
= चिदानंद
यत् (यद्)

Since Sanskrit is 5-10,000 years old, and
most of the writing in it is at least several
hundred years old, many श्लोका:, or parts of them
have been lost, replaced, or have changed. In most
cases, both or all versions convey the same
meaning. When they don't, scholars get something
interesting to argue about!

Although I have used here the words like "books" and "writing", the entire body of the ancient knowledge was faithfully handed down from one generation to the next, for hundreds of years, literally by "word of mouth"!

When several words are joined together to convey a certain meaning, we call this union समास (सम् = together, आस् = to sit), that is, to "sit together'. There are many kinds of समासाः (not the snack समोसा that you may enjoy eating). We will not dwell on this, except to show you a few examples.

करचरण	Hand and foot
कायजम्	Produced by the body
विदितमविदितम्	Known or unknown
मोक्षदायक	Giver of मोक्ष

As you may notice, some words above form a simple couple like करचरण. Other words are joined by a case relationship, like करुणासिंधो. दीनानां शरणं can be joined unchanged as दीनानांशरणं retaining the case-related changes, or as दीनशरणं dropping those changes.

In कायजं, the latter half is a verb, whereas in the rest, it is a noun. There are names for all these kinds of समासाः I We will skip that.

☞ While समास is a union of words, संधि is a union of letters of the alphabet. Words joined as a समास also undergo the appropriate संधि, as we saw in सच्चिदानंद.

Let us review some examples of संधि that you already know. First, the vowels:

अ	+	अ	is	→	आ
अ		इ or ई		→	ए
अ		उ or ऊ		→	ओ

इ or ई		अ		→	य.	दासोस्म्यहम्
उ or ऊ		अ		→	व	(Language)

Now, the consonants:

त्	becomes		→	द् ,	यत् यद्
			→	च्	सच्चिदानंद
ड			→	ज,	Education
क			→	च,	वाक् → वाचा
ट			→	च,	Punctual

And finally, the विसर्ग :

विसर्ग ∎ः	can become 1.	→	Disappear
	2.	→	स्
	3.	→	∎
	4.	→	∎ो

You may recall that the श्लोकाः we looked at were either in the meter अनुष्टुप or in the शार्दूलविक्रीडित. The word for Meter is छंद. You may want to ask someone to show you how to recite these छंदाः melodiously, even though you may not be a talented singer.

If you are planning to throw your arms up and say, "Why should I go on looking for someone to teach me this, or show me that? I have paid for this book!" Hold your horses! I should tell you something about education in traditional India, and in the Sanskrit Era.

A teacher or गुरु has a very special place in the Indian tradition. गुरु gives विद्या (learning, or knowledge). This विद्या is not merely a trade craft or skill. It is a lot more:

सा विद्या या विमुक्तये ।

→ *"The (true) knowledge is that which liberates"*·

सा and या are the feminine forms meaning "She...who".

मुच् = to liberate.

मोक्ष = Salvation.

So the purpose of विद्या is to find one's real self, to be enlightened. Remember, "Know thyself"? गुरु shows you the right way to do that. गुरु may give you a map, but you are the one who has to undertake the journey.

When you need directions, you have to ask several people, till you find your way. It is your duty to find that knowledge. You cannot always buy it either. If you can buy it, it is probably not worth it anyway. So, how do you get that knowledge?

तद्विद्धि प्रणिपातेन → तत् That. विद्या तद्विद्धि (tadviddhi) You obtain प्रणिपातेन by bowing down, by paying respect

परिप्रश्नेन → परि- Around, similar to Peri- (Perimeter, peripheral) प्रश्नेन by questioning प्रश्न = a question

सेवया → by serving सेवा = service.

"(You approach the knowledgeable people, then you) obtain the knowledge from them by paying respect, by asking questions (politely, at the proper time), and by serving them".

Why should they teach you anyway? Real गुरु is not interested in money, yours or otherwise. If you do some work for him, he can easily spare time for you. Why all this? Because,

न हि ज्ञानेन सदृशं पवित्रं इह विद्यते। → *"Indeed, nothing as holy as knowledge exists in this world".*

ज्ञान is knowledge. Sanskrit root verb "Gna" and Latin "Gno" both mean, "to know", as in Agnostic, etc. सदृशं (sad-dri-sham) is "similar". ज्ञानेन सदृशं means "comparable to knowledge". ज्ञानेन is third case singular. With सदृशं, conventionally the third case is used. In English we also say, "in comparison <u>with</u>".

पवित्र	is	Holy, Pure
इह	is	Here, in this world, as opposed to in heaven, or in hell.
विद्यते	is	It Exists.

You may have easily recognized ज्ञानेन as the third case singular, but may have been thrown off by सेवया. It is also the third case singular, but of the feminine gender noun सेवा meaning Service. It is आकारांत feminine noun like सीता, wife of Lord राम, भगवान् रामस्य पत्नी सीता । Let me show you the declensions of सीता. You do remember the eight cases, and three numbers, e.g., singular, etc.

सीता	सीते	सीताः
सीताम्	सीते	सीताः

सीतया	सीताभ्याम्	सीताभिः
सीतायै	सीताभ्याम्	सीतेभ्यः

सीतायाः सीताभ्याम् सीताभ्यः
सीतायाः सीतयोः सीतानाम्

सीतायाम् सीतयोः सीतेषु
हे सीते हे सीते हे सीताः

If you compare these with declensions of राम, an अकारांत masculine noun, you will see many similarities like:

सीताभ्याम्   रामाभ्याम्
सीतानाम्   रामाणाम्

There are some important differences to note as well. You can learn to recognize them by examples. All of the following are in singular number:

First case	सीता (no ∎ः)	रामः
Sixth	सीतायाः	रामस्य
Seventh	सीतये	रामे
Eighth	हे सीते !	हे राम !

We started talking about सीता while discussing how to obtain knowledge.

How do we obtain knowledge? → प्रणिपातेन, परिप्रश्नेन, सेवया.

Let us spend some more time in the company of our गुरु. The word is उकारांत, masculine noun, meaning, "a teacher". As an adjective, it means, "big, or large". Its antonym or opposite is लघु, or "small". Either as a noun, or as an adjective, its declensions are the same.

Let me show you its declensions, again, to point out the similarities.

गुरुः	गुरु	गुरवः
गुरुम्	गुरु	गुरुन्
गुरुणा	गुरुभ्याम्	गुरुभिः
गुरवे	गुरुभ्याम्	गुरुभ्यः
गुरोः	गुरुभ्याम्	गुरुभ्यः
गुरोः	गुर्वोः	गुरुणाम्
गुरौ	गुर्वोः	गुरुषु
हे गुरो !	हे गुरु !	हे गुरवः ।

Once again, you note the similarities. The differences are few.

Sixth case	रामस्य	सीतायाः	गुरोः
Eighth	हे राम !	हे सीते !	हे गुरो !

There are other words similar to गुरु. Do you recall any such उकारांत words?

→ साधु, प्रभु.

147

What is   साधोः in खलस्य साधोः विपरीतमेतद् ?

                                →   Sixth case, singular of साधु.

प्रभो!   →   Eighth case, singular, हे प्रभु!

What is the antonym of गुरु ?   →   लघु

List a few more उकारांत words: →   शंभु
                                       (शिव, शंकर)
                                       सिंधु

Can you think of a few आकारांत names of girls or women?

                                →   उषा, दीपा, आशा, सुलोचना,
                                    Also, डायेना, डोरा, ब्रेन्डा, प्रीसीला, वाना

All these words take the same declensions as सीता. There are many other such nouns that you have came across:

                                →   क्रिया, विद्या, करुणा, काया

List a few अकारांत masculine nouns that you have read in this book, or elsewhere:

                                →   मंत्र, ब्राह्मण, सत्याग्रह, सिंह, हस्त (a hand). Also, ज्योर्ज, पिटर, जीसस,

मोझीस, एब्रहाम,
आइझ्ाक,
वोशिंग्टन.

Thus far we have dealt with nouns and their declensions. We did come across many verbs, and we did learn to recognize the -मि, -सि, and -ति endings for the first, second, and third person respectively.

Verbs are easier to learn. Although, the verbs also have the singular, dual, and the plural numbers, unlike eight cases for the nouns, we have to contend with only three persons, in the case of verbs. Let us take गम् (गच्छ) = to go.

First person	गच्छामि	गच्छावः	गच्छामः
Second	गच्छसि	गच्छथः	गच्छथ
Third	गच्छति	गच्छतः	गच्छन्ति

What does all this mean?

I go	We two go	We go
You go	You two go	You go
He goes	They two go	They go
She goes		
It goes		

These are the conjugations for the present tense. What declensions are for nouns, conjugations are for the verbs. Together, they are called Forms. Here "You go" means "You are going". It is not an order (imperative mood) "You go!" Let me give you a few more verbs.

149

नी (नय्)	to carry
त्यज्	to give up
इष्	to wish (similar, isn't it!)
धाव्	to run
दृश् (पश्य्)	to see
लिख्	to write
विश्	to enter
वद्	to speak
वेद्	to know
पत्	to fall

Of these, you do remember वेद् and दृश् (पश्य्), I am sure. Using the above verbs, try to write in Sanskrit:

I go	→	अहम् गच्छामि ।
I wish	→	अहं इषामि ।
		अहमिषामि ।
		इषाम्यहम् ।
He sees.	→	सः पश्यति ।
She runs.	→	सा धावति ।
It falls.	→	तत् पतति ।
		तत्पतति ।
They write.	→	लिखन्ति ।
(Two girls) enter.	→	विशतः ।
(You two) talk (are talking).	→	वदथः ।

There are some verbs that take a य before undergoing conjugations. For example, कुप् (to get angry) becomes कुप्य.

Write (OK to look up) the conjugations of कुप् ।

→ कुप्यामि कुप्यावः कुप्यामः
कुप्यसि कुप्यथः कुप्यथ
कुप्यति कुप्यतः कुप्यन्ति

Note that -मि, -सि, -ति all are short ि, not the long ones ी.

There are still other verbs that take अय before their conjugations, for example कथ् (to state, to tell). कथयामि means, "I tell".

Write the conjugations of कथ् ।

→ कथयामि कथयावः कथयामः
कथयसि कथयथः कथयथ
कथयति कथयतः कथयन्ति

You do not have to know this, but these य, अय, etc. mark the ten groups or गणाः of the verbs that we talked about earlier. The most important point for you is, we treated all of them alike with

-मि, -सि, or -ति anyway. We have seen verbs from four such गणाः already.

First	गच्छामि	with an	अ	added
Sixth	विशति	with an	अ	added
Fourth	कुप्यति	with a	य	added
Tenth	कथयति	with an	अय	added.

There are six more गणाः just to mention. The verbs of the second गण do not take any such additions. For example, अस् = to be.

अस्मि	स्वः	स्मः
असि	स्थः	स्थ
अस्ति	स्तः	सन्ति

This verb अस् is very irregular. Note that the अ from अस् is seen only in the singular forms of all three persons, that is the extreme left column. Its English counterpart "to be" is also irregular. Let us look at its conjugations:

<u>Am</u>	Are	Are
Are	Are	Are
<u>Is</u>	Are	Are

Write the following in Sanskrit:

I am a teacher.

You are a good person.

अहं गुरुः अस्मि ।
गुरुरस्म्यहम् ।
त्वं साधुः असि ।

She is a girl (बालिका).

सा बालिका अस्ति ।
सा बालिकास्ति ।

The remaining five गणाः (3, 5, 7, 8, and 9) take various other additions. We will not go into all those now, but their -मि, सि, -ति endings will still be same. Verbs from all गणाः also take the same आत्मनेपदी endings, viz., -ए, -से, and -ते as well. Let us take an example: लभ् = to gain, to achieve.

लभे	लभावहे	लभामहे
लभसे	लभेथे	लभध्वे
लभते	लभेते	लभन्ते

This verb is also somewhat irregular, but the basic forms are the same. Just learn to recognize them at a glance. It is not essential at all for you to recognize what गण the verb belongs to, and what addition it has taken. Nor is it necessary for you to memorize which root verb धातु is आत्मनेपदी, परस्मैपदी, or उभयपदी. Their endings will tell you that, if you care to know.

Knowing the गण and पद of a धातु becomes very important, when you want to write something in Sanskrit on your own, or to translate something into Sanskrit from English, for example. Then you have to select the correct additions, if any, and the appropriate endings. However, for reading and understanding what is written, you don't have to know these.

☞   It is very important to be able to recognize the person and the number of a conjugated verb.

In case you are getting impatient, I must point out to you that these गणाः and पदाः can easily and quickly drive you up the wall. We had spent weeks and months, if not years, memorizing them, albeit delightfully, at least in my case.

* * * * * * * * * * * * *

You may want to concentrate on the meaning of verbs. Even if the endings of the root verbs or धातु look somewhat unfamiliar, you can easily identify them as verbs, and recognize their person and number. Now, read the following:

यत्करोषि यदश्नासि
यज्जुहोसि ददासि यत् ।

Can you do the विग्रह of words with संधि, and write them again ?

→ यत् करोषि
यत् अश्नासि
यत् जुहोसि

Which of the words above are verbs? → All four words ending in -सि (षि).

They are all from the गण that we have not covered yet. Still, you could recognize them without any trouble, correct?

→ Say, "Yes" please!

What is यत् ? → "What, which"

यत् यत् = Whatever

What person and number does -सि indicate? → Second, singular

So, the sense of the above lines is.....? → "Whatever you do...", and it lists the four such "whatever"s.

What is the meaning of कृ (कर) ? → To do

दा (यच्छ्) → To give

We did come across these before, when I pointed out the similarity between दान and "Donation". You do not know the other two, but let us try:

अश् → To eat

जुह् → To make an offering into the sacred fire.

यत्तपस्यसि कौन्तेय ! → यत् तपस्यसि कौन्तेय

तत्कुरुष्व मदर्पणम् ॥ → तत् कुरुष्व

मत् अर्पणम्

तपस्यसि → penance and austerities you practice

कुरुष्व → "You do" (an order, the Imperative mood).

From कृ = to do

मत् → To me

अर्पणम् → Offering, dedication.

अर्पण = an offerring.

This श्लोक is from भगवद्गीता, in which Lord कृष्ण tells his friend and disciple prince अर्जुन, son of कुंती (कौन्तेय),

155

"What you do, what you eat, what you offer to the fire, what you give in charity, what penance you practice, dedicate (all) that to Me".

That is, keep your ego out of it, work as my agent, and as a trustee of whatever you have.

If you have followed my advice, and have refrained from memorizing, you have spared yourself a great deal of agony, and have been having good deal of fun along the way.

You must have also learned not to be overwhelmed by, or be intimidated by difficult-looking Sanskrit writings, but rather to break them down into manageably smaller pieces, and to reconstruct their collective meaning. Let us see whether you have.

Read the following श्लोकयुग्म (a couplet):

यदा यदा हि धर्मस्य
ग्लानिर्भवति भारत ।   →   ग्लानिः भवति
अभ्युत्थानमधर्मस्य   →   अभि उत्थानम्
                       अधर्मस्य
तदात्मानं सृजाम्यहम् ॥ १ ॥   →   तदा आत्मानम्
                       सृजामि अहम्

परित्राणाय साधूनां
विनाशाय च दुष्कृताम् ।   →   दुः कृताम्
धर्मसंस्थापनार्थाय   →   धर्म सम् स्थापना
                       अर्थाय

संभवामि युगे युगे ॥ २ ॥

Note the way in which I wrote the stanza numbers ॥ १ ॥ and ॥ २ ॥ above.

Find all the verbs: → भवति, संभवामि, सृजामि.

List various nouns according to their cases: →

१. ग्लानिः अभ्युत्थानम्

२. आत्मानम् दुष्कृताम्

४. परित्राणाय विनाशाय संस्थापनार्थाय

६. धर्मस्य अधर्मस्य

७. युगे युगे

८. भारत !

Now I will arrange the words in modern English order. This order is called अन्वय. It makes it easier to make sense of the content.

हे भारत (born in the भरत dynasty) ! Whenever there is waning ग्लानि of the duties and religion धर्म, and an upsurge अभि + उत्थानम् in misdeeds अ + धर्म, then तदा, I create सृजामि myself अहम् (take birth, Incarnation).

157

For the protection परि + त्राणाय of the good guys साधूनाम्, and च for the destruction of वि + नाशाय the bad deeds (or bad guys) दुष्कृताम्, and for the purpose of अर्थाय (well—) establishing सम् + स्थापना the religion धर्म, I come into being सम् + भवामि in era after era युगे युगे.

This couplet is the most famous one from the गीता. In this couplet, the Lord promises to take birth, if needed, in the interest of good.

How about that! You are reading some very powerful stuff already. There is a lot more to come. You may go back to some of the things we have covered, but there is no need to do that. That will break the continuity, and may make you lose interest.

You can read the entire book again someday, very rapidly. I am trying to give you all the fun, and remove all the torture. However, what is "torture" today may turn out to be "fun" tomorrow !

If you want to memorize a few श्लोकाः or सुभाषितानि, by all means go ahead. If you read them out loud a few times with gusto or spirit, you will by and by remember them automatically. First, understand the meaning of various sayings clearly and correctly. Then you can use them in your conversations with your family and friends.

There is nothing wrong with sharing them with your non-Indian friends either, provided you are sure they care for that. I have a few non-Indian friends, totally unfamiliar with even a word of Sanskrit, who always insist on hearing the original in Sanskrit, and then its meaning in English. These श्लोकाः and especially the सुभाषितानि, are the treasures of the entire human race !

In the first part, we went over the देवनागरी लिपी, including the consonants, vowels, numerals, and the punctuation marks. In the second part, we got acquainted with basic Sanskrit grammar, without ever using that intimidating word.

We looked at the Parts of Speech, e.g., nouns, pronouns, verbs, etc., and familiarized ourselves with their declensions and conjugations. While doing that, we developed a feel for the language, and began to appreciate its charm, beauty, and wisdom acquired through the ages, as expressed in the सुभाषितानि ।

★★★★★★★★★★★★ END PART: II ★★★★★★★★★★★★

....

PART : III
ADVANCED: USING THE POWER TOOLS!

....

The word "Advanced" does not mean that what is yet to come is more difficult to understand, or more complicated. What it does mean is that now you are an advanced student, who is quite familiar with Sanskrit and is ready to have more fun.

In this part, there will be very little that you will find radically different. We will keep on filling the gaps and gradually work to complete the picture. So, sit back, relax, and enjoy.

By now, you have become fluent in reading the देवनागरी लिपी, including all the conjoined consonants, and special characters. You should start reading entire words, rather than one letter or character अक्षर at a time.

As a graduation present to you, I have started to use smaller size Sanskrit अक्षराः । So far, we were using the 24 point size, now we are using the 18 point one. That is still pretty gigantic by any standard. Towards the end of this book, we may graduate to the 12 points, the same size that we have been using for the English text.

We have heard that knowledge is, or gives power. However, power is nothing compared to knowledge, as we can learn from the next सुभाषितम् ।

विद्वत्वं च नृपत्वं च	→	विद्वान् = a scholar The ending -त्वं means "-hood", like motherhood, childhood, etc. विद्वत्वं = learnedness नृप = a king. *"Being learned and being a king..."*
नैव तुल्यं कदाचन ।	→	न एव = never तुल्यं = equal तुला = a weighing scale, balance. कदाचन = ever. *"..are never ever comparable".*
स्वदेशे पूज्यते राजा	→	स्वदेश = own land स्व = self देश = country पूज्यते = is worshipped, from पूज् = to worship. *"(Whereas) a king is respected (only) in his own kingdom..."*
विद्वान् सर्वत्र पूज्यते ॥	→	सर्वत्र = everywhere अत्र = here तत्र = there. सर्व = All *"a scholar is honored everywhere".*

You are not expected to be able to answer this, but what can you tell me about पूज्यते ?

→ धातु पूज्,
Fourth गण (य added),
आत्मनेपदी (-ते ending),
third person, singular.

Should this verb belong to other गणाः, how would it look?

First गण ?	→ पूजते	(अ added)
Sixth	→ पूजते	(अ added)
Tenth	→ पूजयते	(अय added)
Second	→ पूज्ते or पूत्ते.	(Nothing added)

All these forms are only for illustration, and are of course incorrect, except पूज्यते ।

Can you re-write the following, after doing the विग्रह (opposite of संधि) ?

सत्यमेव जयते नानृतम्। → सत्यम् एव जयते न अनृतम् ।

This saying means, *"The truth (alone) prevails, not the lie !"* सत्यमेव जयते is the slogan which appears on official Indian seals, under a likeness of three-lion-heads. It is the Indian equivalent of *"E Pluribus Unum"* i.e., "We are many, let us be one".

Can you identify the word(s) that mean:

Only	→ एव
Prevails	→ जयते

जि (जय्) = to win.
You may know people named जय, विजय, जयेश, जया, etc.

Truth, Verity	→	सत्यम्
		Like वनम्, first case, singular, neuter.

A lie	→	अनृतम्

Take another one-liner:

एकं सद्विप्रा बहुधा वदंति ।	→	एकम् सत् विप्राः बहुधा वदन्ति ।

What it means is, *"The truth is one, the wisemen say it differently".*

What is	सत्?	→	सत्य. Truth.
	एकम्	→	One.
			एकवचन = singular
	Many	→	बहु. बहुवचन = plural
	बहुधा	→	In many, various ways This is an Adverb.
	विप्राः	→	विप्र = a Brahmin, विप्राः = Brahmins.

ब्राह्मण (scholars), क्षत्रिय (warriors), वैश्य (merchants), and शूद्र (servants, including the janitors, butchers, and other "untouchables") were the four castes in ancient India. ब्राह्मणः were the students and keepers of scriptures and other knowledge, and hence were considered to be wise.

We have come across a few pairs of antonyms or opposites. Can you recall any of them?

	→	एक	बहु
		लघु	गुरु
		साधु	खल

We also saw a few words that do not undergo any conjugations or declensions. What are they called?

	→	अव्यय

What is अन्वय? → Arranging the words in a modern order to facilitate understanding their meaning.

What does अव्यय include (answer in English)? → Prepositions, Conjunctions, Interjections, and Adverbs.

Give a few examples of Prepositions (English): → To, For, From, Of, Behind, Under, etc.

How do we handle these in Sanskrit? → We use cases e.g., रामं, रामेण, रामाय, etc.

List Sanskrit Conjunctions: → च (and), वा (or)

Can you list a few Sanskrit Interjections? → भो! हे! रे!

Any Sanskrit Adverbs (time, place, manner)? → यदा (when)
तदा (then)

यथा (how)
तथा (in that manner)

एवम् (thus)
प्रति (towards)
बहुधा, अत्र, तत्र, सर्वत्र.

In the previous part, we looked at five गणाः of verbs, viz., First, Second, Fourth, Sixth, and Tenth.

What are First, Fifth, etc. called in English? → Ordinal Numbers. They indicate Order.

What are Cardinal numbers? → One, two, three, etc.

Can you list and say the देवनागरी numerals? →   ०.   शून्य   (Read on)

This is a very important numeral and number. It not only means "Zero" or "nothing", but it represents by virtue of being a full circle, the entirety, completeness, perfection, etc. in mystic sciences. In the conventional sense of being "nothing', it does not always mean "worthless', but rather, a high level of austerity, graced by a total lack of possessions.

→   १.   एक
२.   द्वि
३.   त्रि
४.   चतुर्
५.   पंच

You are familiar with एकवचन,   द्विवचन, and बहवचन. द्वि is similar to Di, and त्रि is exactly same as Tri. You may recall the words वाक् and वाचा to see how "K" becomes "Ch". Now, चतुर् may not look too different from Quatro. A fruit punch contains five juices, and when we punch someone, we use all five fingers.

→   ६.   षष्
७.   सप्त
८.   अष्ट
९.   नव
१०. दश

Two trangles, ਠ ਠ in षष् make six lines to remind you of the number it stands for.

If you know Spanish or Latin, you can see the similarity with S<u>ept</u>ember, O<u>cto</u>ber, <u>Nove</u>mber, and <u>Dece</u>mber, for ७-८-९-१०. As you know very well, I am sure, Emperors Julius Caesar and Augustus added two months bearing their names, pushing these months by two counts to 9-12. Their original, and now incorrect names still remain.

Now, let us look at the Ordinal Numbers, like First, Second, etc. There is of course no Ordinal Number for Zero. We never say "Zeroeth House", etc.

First	प्रथम	→	"Primum" in Latin
Second	द्वितीय		
Third	तृतीय		

-ईय is commonly used to make an adjective. Remember, all numbers are adjectives, since they modify nouns. A cow, five cows, the third cow.

Fourth	चतुर्थः	Here, -th ending is applied. "Quart" is one-fourth of a gallon.
Fifth	पंचमः	
Sixth	षष्टः	

From now on, we will apply the equivalent of -th, which is -मः, to obtain Ordinal Numbers.

Seventh	सप्तमः
Eighth	अष्टमः
Ninth	नवमः
Tenth	दशमः

From now on, it gets very easy. To obtain any Ordinal Number, we just apply -म to the corresponding Cardinal Number.

The Sanskrit word for a part or a fraction is अंश. We can easily derive the fractions by applying the ending -अंश to the Ordinal Numbers. Let us get the only exception out of the way.

"A half" is called अर्ध. It is one of the two parts, so we call it एक द्वितीय अंश or एक द्वितीयांश.

167

You may try these:

One half	→	एक द्वितीयांश, अर्ध
One fourth	→	एक चतुर्थांश
One seventh	→	एक सप्तमांश
One fifth	→	एक पंचमांश
Five sixth	→	पंच षष्टांश
Nine tenth	→	नव दशांश

Note that the numerator is not changed. The -th or -अंश is applied only to the denominator. This is not a rule. It is an observation.

* * * * * * * * * * * *

We noted the similarity between Sept-Octo-Nov-Dec and सप्त, अष्ट, नव, दश, etc. There are innumerable such similarities between Sanskrit and European languages. The British scholars and others who came to colonial India in the eighteenth century were highly impressed by these similarities. They conceived the idea that Sanskrit, Latin, English, and other languages, have an original common ancestor.

This suggested ancestor has not been found to date. However, these languages, together with many of their daughter languages are collectively called "Indo-European Languages". If English is your mother tongue, Sanskrit is your aunt, and if your mother tongue is Gujarati, Marathi, Hindi, or any of the north Indian tongues, then Sanskrit is the grandmother! The Indo-European languages are spoken by nearly two-thirds (द्वि तृतीयांश) of the population of the world.

You may want to contrast the way in which you are learning Sanskrit, with the way Sir William Jones did. Sir William Jones, a Briton appointed as a judge of the Calcutta high court, was deeply interested in Indian culture and languages. He approached a ब्राह्मण scholar from the holy city काशी or वाराणसी (Banaras).

At first the scholar flatly refused to teach the divine language to a meat-eating, wine-drinking, westerner. Sir Jones had to "purify" himself, his house, etc. and keep it that way by washing it with milk for the duration of the study spanning at least a few months.

Finally, when the tutoring did begin, the scholar did not know a word of English, and he would not degrade his tongue by speaking in the "non-divine and perverted" modern Indian dialects somewhat comprehensible to Sir Jones. He would only speak in Sanskrit which Sir Jones did not know a word of. You can imagine the rest of the story.

A few months later, Sir William Jones wrote an article about the similarities among the languages of the world, and coined the term "Indo-European Family of Languages"! Anybody else would have given up trying to learn संस्कृत, but not Sir William Jones. There is a good सुभाषितम् about such साधु people:

प्रारभ्यते न खलु विघ्नभयेन नीचैः →

प्र + आ + रभ् = to begin
विघ्न = obstacle +
भयेन = danger
विघ्नस्य भयेन = by the fear of (anticipated) obstacle
नीच = the worst kind,
खलु = indeed

"Being afraid of the anticipated obstacles, the lowly kind of people do not even begin a task"

If you care to see a little poetic beauty, note that the construction of this first line is in a Passive Voice. Literally, it says,

"Indeed, by the worst kind of people, afraid of dangers of obstacles (to come), (the work) is not even started".

This brings out the apathy of this kind of people in stark contrast to the better ones, who actively get involved.

प्रारभ्य विघ्नविहता विरमन्ति मध्याः । → प्रारभ्य = having begun
विघ्नेन विहताः thwarted
विघ्न. वि + हन् = to kill, to destroy
विरमन्ति = They give up.
वि + रम् = to rest.
मध्य = middle.
"Having begun a task, the average people abndon it, when con-fronted with hurdles".

विघ्नैः पुनः पुनरपि प्रतिहन्यमाना → पुनः = again
अपि = but, even then
पुनः अपि, पुनर् अपि,
पुनरपि again and again
प्रति- Re-, opposite
हन् = to kill, hurt.
प्रतिहन्यमानाः = (those who are) forced back, being hurt

"(However, even when) faced with obstacles over and over again..."

प्रारब्धमुत्तमजना न परित्यजन्ति ॥　　→　प्रारब्धम् उत्तम जनाः न परित्यजन्ति ॥

प्रारब्धम् = begun.
Past participle.
त्यज् = to abandon
न परित्यजन्ति = 'they do not give up"

"Once having begun, the best ones do not give up!"

Read the whole श्लोकः again. It is not in the meter अनुष्टुप, nor in शार्दूलविक्रीडित. It is in a meter called वसंततिलका. I have asked you before to find someone who can demonstrate how to sing various meters, or how to pronounce certain words, declensions, संधि, etc.

Why don't I prepare an audio cassette or a CD? Maybe I will, some day! There is no knowledge without a teacher, and one teacher may not be able to teach you everything.

The quest for a गुरु is an eternal quest, lasting for several lifetimes, according to the Indian tradition. Books can only give you information. For knowledge, you need a गुरु ।

In the last सुभाषित, we came across the words खलु and अपि, meaning, "indeed" and "but" respectively. They are अव्ययाः and you may want to add them to your list of अव्ययाः ।

We also came across the words प्रारभ्य, प्रारब्ध, हन्यमानाः, and विहता । These words do not have the familiar endings like -मि, -सि, or -ति, etc. Nor do they seem like declensions of राम, सीता, गुरु, etc.

Can you recall their meanings?

प्रारभ्य	→	having begun
प्रारब्ध	→	(what is) begun
हन्यमानाः	→	(those) being hurt
विहता	→	(who are) confronted

Can you name the eight parts of speech in English?

→ Noun, Pronoun, Adjectives, Verbs, Adverbs, Prepositions, Conjunctions, Interjections.

To which part of speech do the above words belong?

→ None really, but they do appear to behave like some of them.

That is correct. What parts of speech do they apparently belong to?

प्रारभ्य	→	an adverb
प्रारब्ध	→	a noun
हन्यमानाः	→	an adjective
विहताः	→	an adjective

They are indeed used as adjectives, adverbs, nouns, etc. However, they are derived from verbs.

Can you recall the verbs of their origin?

प्रारभ्य	→	प्र + आ + रभ्
प्रारब्ध	→	प्र + आ + रभ्

हन्यमानाः → हन्

विहता → वि + हन्

So, these words are originally verbs, but are not verbs. They are "Part-verbs", or Participles. You are quite familiar with Past Participles in English.

Give the past Participles of the followings:

Go	went	→	gone
Do	did	→	done
Eat	ate	→	eaten
Put	put	→	put

विहत and प्रारब्ध are past participles. Like "gone" and "done", they mean, "confronted" and "begun". They are then used as adjective-like nouns, and they undergo the same declensions as nouns, e.g., राम or सीता, etc.

From हन् (to hurt, to kill), हन्यमान् is the present partciple, meaning, "one who is being hurt or killed". प्रारभ्य is a participle used as an adverb. Participles are easy to recognize.

A short while ago, we looked at Prefixes like Pre- or प्र-, and we saw them applied to verbs or to other words.

What are the Prefixes called? → पूर्वग
(which goes before)

What are they called, when they are applied to verbs?

→ उपसर्ग

The verbs with उपसर्ग like प्र+आ+रभ् are called सोपसर्ग (स + उपसर्ग, i.e., with उपसर्ग). These verbs and

173

those without an उपसर्ग differ in the way they form
participles. Don't worry. You won't be doing this.
You will see this only after it is already done.

Examples of सोपसर्ग Verbs forming participles:

नि + हन्	निहत्य	→	having killed
प्र + आ + रभ्	प्रारभ्य	→	having begun
उत् + यम्	उत्यम्य, उद्यम्य	→	उत् = Up
			यम् = to try
			having lifted

Verbs without an उपसर्ग :

गम्	गत्वा	→	having gone
हन्	हत्वा	→	having killed
यम्	यत्वा	→	having tried
वच्	उच् + त्वा, उक् + त्वा		
	उक्त्वा	→	having spoken.
			उ and व are close,
			remember, Lang<u>uage</u>?
What is the meaning of	गत्वा ?	→	having gone
	गत	→	gone
	हत्वा	→	having slain
	हत	→	killed
	हन्यमान्	→	(who is) being killed

गत्वा, प्रारभ्य are used as adverbs, and hence are
treated as अव्यय. They do not change. On the other
hand, गत, हन्यमान् are used as nouns, and hence they
do undergo declensions.

There are several more participles. One
commonly used form is कर्तुम्, ज्ञातुम् ("for doing", "for
knowing") from धातु कृ, and ज्ञा (जान्) meaning, "to do"
and "to know". They indicate purpose or intention.
Since they are adverbs of purpose, they do not
undergo any declensions either.

The participles are called कृदंत, in case you wanted to know. Even if you did not, it is useful to know the various endings of these कृदंताः । You learn these only once, and then their sense is always obvious to you, even when you do not know the original verb or धातु.

In as much as no work is involved on your part, let us look at one more group of कृदंताः । They convey advice in the form of "should or must be done". There is no compulsion here. What is implied is duty, or propriety. Such कृदंताः are recognizable by their -य, -तव्य, -अनीय endings. All three convey the same meaning, with only slightly different flavor.

Let us apply these endings to the verb कृ, meaning, "to do" :

करणीय	worth doing
कर्तव्य	mission, duty
कार्य	work, deed

An example will make it clear:

यद्यपि सत्यं लोकविरुद्धं   →

	यदि अपि सत्यं	
यदि	=	Even
अपि	=	but
यद्यपि	=	even though
लोक	=	people
विरुद्धं	=	against
वि+रुह्		to oppose

ना करणीयं नाचरणीयम् ।   →

ना		(negative)
करणीयम्		be done
आचरणीयम्	आ+चरणीयम्	
चर्	=	to practice
		to walk (on a path).

175

आचरण = conduct
चरण = leg.

"Even though it may appear to be the right course of action, should it be against the accepted norms, it should not be done, should not be practised".

List all the forms of कृदंताः you know: → करणीय, कार्य, कर्तव्य, कर्तुम्, हत्वा, गत, प्रारभ्य, प्रारब्ध, निहत्य

Let us leave the part-verbs or participles, and return to the verbs themselves. As I promised, in this part we will go over our un-finished business, without really any work on your part.

As we saw earlier, verbs from different गणाः take different additions, before undergoing conjugations. You may recall that either the verbs may not take any such addition, or may take अ, य, or अय. There are other additions, like न, नु, उ, ना, or the end part of the verb may be duplicated.

Just look at these. Don't worry about their meaning. That will come when we use these verbs. Write the meaning, if you know it:

दा (यच्छ्)	ददाति	→	To give. Note the duplication of द.
शु	शृणोति	→	To hear. नु added
रुह्	रुणध्धि	→	To rise. न added.
तन्	तनोति	→	To spread. उ added.
क्री	क्रीणाति	→	To play. ना added.

The above was only for illustration. We went over that quickly. You do not have to remember these, but I have listed the various additions that distinguish various गणाः ।

176

१.	वदामि	अ
२.	अस्मि	None
३.	ददासि	Duplication
४.	पूज्यते	य
५.	श्रृणोति	नु, उ became ओ
६.	विशति	अ, same as first गण.
७.	रुणधि	न
८.	तनोति	उ, उ became ओ
९.	क्रीणाति	ना
१०.	कथयति	अय

The most important part for you is to recognize -मि, -ति, -न्ति, etc. We have already seen many such verbs, and you had no difficulty with them. You may recall the following:

यत्करोषि यदश्नासि
यज्जुहोसि ददासि यत् ।

"Whatever you do, eat, offer to the fire, give to charity (dedicate all that to Me)".

There are four verbs there, as identifiable with their -सि or -षि ending. That indicates second person, "you".

Which verb contains a duplication?	→	ददासि
Which verb has ना added to it?	→	अश्नासि
Which verb has उ (ओ) added to it?	→	करोषि, जुहोसि
What is यज्जुहोसि ?	→	यत् जुहोसि

For our purpose, it is more important to know the person, number, and meaning if we can. Knowing which गण the verb belongs to is good and desirable, but it is not necessary for reading or understanding. For writing correctly, of course, you have to know that.

For the same reason, you don't have to know whether the verb is आत्मनेपदी or परस्मैपदी, or उभयपदी, until you start writing in संस्कृत. Our purpose is reading, comprehension, and *appreciation without any apprehension*. You will remember the words by their usage and context.

* *

Let us now turn our attention to nouns. We have left them alone for a long time. Since I am not asking you to do anything, I am sure you won't mind what follows. We did cover the following nouns:

Masculine राम   गुरु
Feminine   सीता
Neuter वन

Which of the above are अकारांत ?   →   राम, वन
What -अंत (ending) is गुरु ?   →   उ-कारांत
                  सीता ?   →   आ-कारांत

Now, let me show you the full range of nouns with all their various अंताः (endings) ।

M	राम	गुरु	कलि		नेतृ	गो	
F.	सीता	धेनु	मति	नदी वधू	मातृ	गो	नौ
N.	वन	मधु	वारि				

All the above end in a vowel. You can see the अ, आ, उ, ऊ, ओ, औ endings. Which is the vowel ending in नेतृ and in मातृ ?

            →   ऋ. with "Ri" sound.

There are other nouns that end in a consonant, rather than in a vowel. The verb has to end in a half consonant, because otherwise it will end in a vowel ! No reason for you to worry at all. Look at the following verbs:

M.   मरुत् सुहद् -च्   -ज् -श् शशिन् राजन् विद्वस् चंद्रमस्
F.   महत् आपद् दिश्   करिन् सीमन्
N.   जगत्   भाविन्   पयस्

One reason I am showing you all these is to impress upon you how much agony you have been spared. Along with torture and agony, albeit, some fun is also lost. I recall studying all these declensions with a great deal of fun, which I hope you will also have some day. Certainly not now.

The words महत् and करिन् from the feminine gender verbs are routinely converted into महती and करिणी, and then are declined as नदी. Note the spelling महती, rather than महति ! The latter is for verbs, in third person singular.

Similarly, आपद् is declined as a masculine word सुहद् ! and सीमन् as राजन् ! Also, all masculine and feminine nouns with -च्, -ज्, -श् endings are all declined as दिश् ! Look at how much you have been spared.

You will get to know these by and by. Their declensions are more similar than different from राम, सीता, वन, and गुरु. Let us see them in use:

शशिना च निशा निशया च शशि   →   शशिन् = Moon
                                     निशा = night
शशिना निशया च विभाति नभः ।   →   नभस् = sky
                                     वि + भा to be adorned

What is विभाति ?   →   It looks beautiful.

Can you guess the meaning of this श्लोकार्ध ?   →   *"By Moon, the night, by night, the Moon, by the moon and the night, the sky looks beautiful !"*

What case is शशिना and निशया ?   →   Third case, singular. <u>By</u> or <u>with</u>.

What case is नभः ?   →   First. <u>It</u> looks good.

What is the first case declension of Moon and of Night?

       →   शशि, निशा.

Let us complete this lovely stanza.

पयसा कमलं कमलेन पयः   →   पयस् = water
                                   कमल = Lotus

पयसा कमलेन विभाति सरः ॥   →   सरस् = Lake

These lines are patterned after the first two lines. Can you guess what does it say?

       →   *"By water, the lotus, by lotus, the water, by lotus and water the lake looks lovely"!*

Which nouns are in the   first case?   →   कमलं, पयः, सरः
                                third   →   कमलेन, पयसा

It is a very delightful श्लोकः with a pleasant and tranquill mood. Its rhythm or cadence is also soothing, like the water-scape and the sky-scape it describes.

So, the next time you see रामेण, सीतया, पयसा, शशिना, etc., you will know immediately that they are referring to the third case singular form of the noun, not by reading this dull paragraph, but because you have read the delightful शशिना च निशा......सरः !

To refresh your memory, without taxing it, you will recall,

विद्वान् सर्वत्र पूज्यते ।   →   *"A scholar is revered everywhere"*.
विद्वान् is the first case singular of विद्वस् ।

जगतः पितरौ वंदे पार्वतीपरमेश्वरौ ।   →

जगतः	=	Of the
जगत्	=	world
पितरौ	=	parents
पितृ	=	father
मातृ	=	mother
भ्रातृ	=	brother
दुहितृ	=	daughter

Note the similarity.

The above lines, जगतः पितरौ वंदे पार्वतीपरमेश्वरौ are from the poem रघुवंश, the story of the dynesty रघु, an ancestor of राम. It was composed by the great poet कालिदास. He lived in the fourth century and is often compared to Shakespeare. His another famous poem is कुमारसंभव, about the birth (संभव), of Lord शंकरस्य child (कुमार), named कार्तिकेय, created to destroy the evil असुराः।

The next line is from the कुमारसंभव,

अस्त्युत्तरस्यां दिशि देवतात्मा   →   अस्ति उत्तरस्याम्

अस्ति	=	i s
अस्	=	to be

हिमाल्यो नाम नगाधिराजः । →

उत्तर	=	North
दिशि	=	in the-
दिश्	=	direction

देवता आत्मा

देवता	=	gods
आत्मा	=	soul
हिम	=	snow, ice
आल्य	=	abode
नाम	=	name(d)
नग	=	न + गच्छति

"does not go" mountain

अधिराज	a king

"In the North, there is a great mountain, pure white like a divine soul, named Himalaya (an abode of snow)."

We saw examples of दिश्, शशिन्, पयस्, जगत्, विद्वस्, पितृ, etc., in the beginning of the previous section, and we came across the word महत् also. To refresh your memory,

यथा चित्तं तथा वाचा
यथा वाचा तथा क्रिया ।
चित्ते वाचि क्रियायां च
महतामेकरूपता ॥

In case you have forgotten, this सुभाषितम् states that, *"For the great ones, there prevails uniformity among their mind, speech, and action".*

महत् means great or big. You have heard words like महात्मा (the great soul), महाराजा (the great king), and महावीर (the great victor, Lord Mahavir).

* * * * * * * * * * * * * *

182

Now read the following prayer to Lord राम.

आपदामपहर्तारं   →   आपदाम् अपहर्तारम्

अप + हृ (हर्)

     =   to remove

हर्तृ (Hartru)

     =   Remover

दातारं सर्व संपदाम् ।   दातृ   =   giver

संपद्   =   wealth

लोकाभिरामं श्री रामं   →   लोक अभिरामं

भूयो भूयो नमाम्यहम् ॥   →   भूयः भूयः नमामि अहम्

भूयः   =   again

*"I bow again and again, to Lord
Ram, remover of woes, giver of wealth,
and giver of bliss to people."*

Can you find any अव्यय ?   →   भूयः

What is   संपदाम् ?   →   Of wealth

                   आपदाम् ?   →   Of woes

What are the adjectives used for राम ?   →   अपहर्तारम् (आपदाम्)

दातारम् (सर्व संपदाम्)

लोकाभिरामम्

What case are they in?   →   Second. I bow <u>to</u>

What is श्री (रामम्) ?   →   श्री   = Revered, Mr.

☞   श्री is a condensed form of श्रीमत् and
hence, in हिन्दी and in मराठी, two modern Indian
languages derived from संस्कृत, it is written
with a period, thus: श्री. The feminine form
Mrs. is श्रीमती, which is not abbreviated.

Now we have seen the words आपद् , हर्तृ, दातृ,
संपद्, etc.

* * * * * * * * * * * * *

183

Read the following सुभाषितम् ।

उदये सविता रक्तो
रक्तश्चास्तमने तथा ।   →   रक्तः च अस्तमने तथा
                                              श्च is श्च, श् + च
                                              अस्तमने =   at sunset

संपत्तौ च विपत्तौ च
महतामेकरूपता ॥   →   महताम् एकरूपता

What is महताम् एकरूपता ?   →   "Of the great ones,
                                              (is) uniformity"

Where have we heard that before?   →   चित्ते वाचि क्रियायां च....॥

What is   तथा ?   →   "and", च

                     उदये   →   उदय =   Rise
                                              Seventh case, while
                                              rising, in good times

                     सविता   →   first case of
                                              सवितृ =   the Sun

                     रक्त   →   Red. Literally, blood.

                     संपत्तौ   →   in wealth, good times

                     विपत्तौ   →   in bad times

> "Either at Sunrise or at Sunset,
> the Sun is always red. (Indeed), in good
> times or in bad ones, the great ones are
> always the same."

Can you find two pairs of antonyms (opposites) ?

                                      →   संपत्   विपत्
                                              उदय   अस्त

What is the opposite of "antonym"?   →   synonym

What is   सूर्य + उदय ?   →   सूर्योदय   Sunrise
                     सूर्य + अस्त   →   सूर्यास्त   Sunset

* * * * * * * * * * *

184

Suppose we want to say that the Sun is "more red" at Sunrise, than at Sunset. We may want to say "most red" or "the reddest" also. Let us go back to English.

What are "more" and "most" called ?   →   The Degrees of Comparison
"More" is comparative
"Most" is superlative

"More" compares any two things, while "Most" compares many and indicates a comparison with all the rest.

Write the superlative degrees of the following:

Good	Better	→	Best
Fast	Faster	→	Fastest
Dark	Darker	→	Darkest
Near	Nearer	→	Nearest, Next
Little	Littler, Less	→	Littlest, Least

In संस्कृत, we use -तर for comparative, and -तम for the superlative degree. You may want to try this:

रक्त	Red	रक्ततर	→	रक्ततम	
उच्च	High	उच्चतर	→	उच्चतम,	
				उत्तम =	the Best
सुंदर	Beautiful	सुंदरतर	→	सुंदरतम	
शीतल	Cold	शीतलतर	→	शीतलतम	
उष्ण	Hot	उष्णतर	→	उष्णतम	

☞   Unlike English, in संस्कृत such degrees of comparison are used with verbs also.

An example will be "Early bird (more likely) gets the worm". लभ् means, "to get, to achieve". The

185

same -तर and -तम endings are applied with a minor change. We apply -तराम् and -तमाम् instead.

| लभते | लभतेतराम् | → | लभतेतमाम् |

| What is लभते ? | → | He / She /It achieves third person singular आत्मनेपदी. |

Another example:

प्रयत्नं सततं कुर्वाणो	→	प्रयत्न =	effort
		प्र + यत्	to try
		सततं =	continuous
		कुर्वाण =	doer, from
		कुर्वत् =	"doing"
		present participle of	
		कृ =	to do
संपदं लभतेतराम् ।	→	(You know this).	
संपदं लभते नरः । This is another version.	→	नर =	a man
		नारी =	a woman
		नृ is the root word.	

What is	संपद्?	→	Wealth, success
	लभतेतराम्	→	more likely to succeed
	लभतेतमाम्	→	most likely to succeed

Literally, *"the continuously striving one is more likely to succeed"*. It is always the (slow, but) steady that is more likely to win".

There is more than one way to show that one thing is better than another. You may recall,

| सर्पदुर्जनयोर्मध्ये | | | |
| वरं सर्पो न दुर्जनः । | → | वरं = | Better |

We can achieve the same by using the word "better" or गरीयस् itself. Its declensions (as if you are going to do this) are similar to those of विद्वस् ।

Can you guess the feminine form of गरीयस्?

→ गरीयसी, (गरीयसा)

गरीयसी is correct. I suppose, if the original word was गरीयस, instead of गरीयस्, then the आकारांत form might have been correct.

Do you know any other ई-कारांत feminine noun?

→ नदी = a river

Read this:

जननी जन्मभूमिश्च

→ भूमिश्च = भूमिः च भूमिश्च

भूमि = land

स्वर्गादपि गरीयसी ।

→ स्वर्ग = heaven

What is the meaning of स्वर्गाद् ?

→ स्वर्गात्= Of, from, (here, it is "than")

अपि → but

What is the root word of जननी, and
जन्म ? → जन् (जा)

What does जन् (जा) mean? → To be born. Like, "Gen", Genetics, Hydrogen".

जननी → Mother
जन्म → Birth
जन्मभूमि → Land of one's birth

This श्लोकार्ध (half Shlok) means,

"One's mother, and Motherland, are more preferred than heaven!"

Which of the following is incorrect?

जननी च जन्मभूमिः च → This is correct.

जननी जन्मभूमिः च → Can't be this. That's how it is written in the present example.

जननी च जन्मभूमि → This is incorrect.

In English, the last one would be the only correct way. We say, "you and I". In Sanskrit, we say either, "you, I and", or "you and, I and". That poor ब्राह्मण गुरु of Sir William Jones would have had a hard time understanding, why Sir William Jones could not get even such a simple thing right!

* *

Now let us read this:

न चैतद्विद्मः कतरन्नो गरीयो → द् + व, द् + म. "Chaitdvidmah"

It may look intimidating, but let us divide and then conquer it.

न च एतद् विद्मः →

न	=	Nor
च	=	And
एतद्	=	This
विद्	=	to know

What is विद्मः ? → Go back to गम् (गच्छ)

Let us look at conjugations of गम् (गच्छ). Their first person forms go like this:

गच्छामि   गच्छावः   गच्छामः

विद्मः ?

Is that so? विद् belongs to the second गण, and its conjugations go like:

वेद्मि   विद्वः   विद्मः

So, what does विद्मः mean?   →   "We (all) know".

There are four ancient Books of Knowledge, or वेदाः । They are ऋग्वेदः, सामवेदः, यजुर्वेदः, and अथर्ववेदः। Not included among these is a somewhat modern आयुर्वेदः, which is a treatise on Medicine. आयु = Life, longevity.

The श्लोकः under discussion, न चैतद्विद्मः...is from भगवन्गीता. It expresses the soul wrenching dilemma of अर्जुन, who is faced with choosing between one, killing his unjust first cousins supported by their common relatives, and two, sparing his cousins, and thereby putting up with the injustice.

I will give you the entire श्लोकः, without going into the details. Its meaning will follow.

न चैतद्विद्मः कतरन्नो गरियो
यद्वा जयेम यदि वा नो जयेयुः ।
यानेव हत्वा न जिजिविषामः
तेऽवस्थिता प्रमुखे धार्तराष्ट्राः ॥

"We know not what is better for us,
nor do we know whether they would
win, or we will.
Having killed whom, we may not want
to live,
they are the ones, the sons of धृतराष्ट्र,
who are confronting us!"

कतरम्	Which is better
नः or नो	to, or for us
गरीयो	गरीयस् → गरीयः → गरीयो
एतद्	This

* *

PRONOUNS:

In the above, we saw some pronouns, e.g. नः or नो, यत्, ते, etc. Some of these are declensions of basic pronouns. One pronoun can replace many nouns, and are therefore good to know. A list of them follows:

अस्मद्	I
युष्मद्	You
तत्	He / She / It
एतद्	This
यत्	Which
किम्	What
सर्व	A l l

You may complain that you do not see many pronouns here that are familiar to you. Do you know why not?

→ Because the familiar ones are declensions of these basic pronouns.

From	अस्मत्	अहम्, नः, नो	→	Compare <u>No</u>sotros
	युष्मत्	त्वम्, वः, वो	→	Compare <u>Vo</u>sotros, in Spanish.
	तत्	सः, सा, तत्	→	He, She, It

Personal Pronouns, Singular:

यां चिन्तयामि सततं मयि सा विरक्ता
साप्यन्यमिच्छति जनं स जनोऽन्यसक्तः ।　　→　सा अपि अन्यम् इच्छति
　　　　　　　　　　　　　　　　　　जनः अन्य सक्तः

अस्मत्कृते च परितुष्यति काचिदन्या　　→　अस्मद् कृते
　　　　　　　　　　　　　　　　　　काचिद् = Someone
　　　　　　　　　　　　　　　　　　अन्य = another
　　　　　　　　　　　　　　　　　　अन्या = ,, woman

धिक् तां च तं च मदनं च इमां च मां च ॥　→　धिक् ! Shows contempt
　　　　　　　　　　　　　　　　　　मदन = Eros

The underlined words may not look familiar to you, but are worth knowing. They can be very useful to you. They are various forms of personal pronouns, viz., I, You, He/She/It, etc.

Also included are "Some, the other, Another, That, All, etc.". This latter group, when it is used for inanimate things, understandably, it does not remain "personal" any longer.

They are used extremely commonly. Therefore, you will learn to recognize them easily. Each pronoun has its declensions covering all seven cases. Yes, only seven, not eight.

☞　　There is no Vocative case for address for pronouns. There is no usage such as "Hey, Me!", or "Hey, He/She/It !", or "Hey, You !" either. In the last instance, you simply use the noun, rather than the pronoun.

For now, pay attention to their second case singular forms given below. Then try to find them in the above सुभाषितम् ।

1st Person ("I") or अस्मद् : माम् (मा)　　To me → अस्मत्कृते
　　　　　　　　　　　　　　　　　　　　　"from my doing"

2nd Person ("You) or युष्मत् : त्वाम् (त्वा) To you

3rd Person or

("He/She/It") or तत् : ... .

Masculine ("He"):	तम्	To him
Feminine ("She"):	ताम्	To her
Neuter ("It"):	तद्	To it

This सुभाषितम् was written by a king भर्तृहरि in a collection of one hundred (शत) श्लोकाः on worldly wisdom (नीति), called नीतिशतक. He has also written शतकाः on शृंगार ("Sex"), विज्ञान (spiritual science), and on वैराग्य (detachment from the world).

They are now almost two thousand years old. The king was very good, and infidelity was a norm for kings. His teacher or गुरु saw that, fallen deeply in love with his queen, the king was ignoring his duties to himself and to his kingdom.

To bring him back to the path of duty, the गुरु set him up for disillusionment and eventual detachment. The queen was chaste, and is still highly regarded, as is the गुरु.

The king भर्तृहरि received the Fruit of Immortality, which he gave to his beloved queen, who gave to her lover the chief of cavalry, who gave it to another woman whom he loved. The latter was in love with the king himself, and gave the fruit back to him. भर्तृहरि saw through what was happening. Now read:

"The woman whom (यां) I am always contemplating, she (सा) is not interested in me (मयि).

She also (सा अपि) desires another (अन्यम्) person. He (सः) is attached to (yet) another (अन्या) woman.

From (in) my actions (अस्मद् कृते) is satisfied that some (काचिद्) other woman (अन्या).

Contempt be to her (the queen) (ताम्), and to that man (तम्), and to the god of love (मदन), and to that woman, (इमाम्) and to myself (माम्) as well !"

Pay particular attention to the fourth or the last line, and say it out loud a few times to appreciate the soft nasal sounds alternating with the teeth grating harsh च sounds, and deepening the expression of contempt.

The Most Important Person — "I"

Whenever we speak, it is usually to express our self-centered observations and viewpoint. We are the center of our universe. I have given below all declensions of "I" just for you to look at.

अस्मद् ("I")

Case	Singular	Dual	Plural
१.	अहम्	आवाम्	वयम्
२.	माम् (मा)	आवाम् (नौ)	अस्माकम् (नः)
३.	मया	आवाभ्याम्	अस्माभिः
४.	मह्यम् (मे)	आवाभ्याम् (नौ)	अस्मभ्यम् (नः)
५.	मत्	आवाभ्याम्	अस्मत्
६.	मम (मे)	आवयोः (नौ)	अस्माकम् (नः)
७.	मयि	आवयोः	अस्मासु

☞ As we noted earlier, there is no eighth case for pronouns.

☞ The forms in the parentheses are optional ones, and are never used at the beginning of a sentence.

☞ You won't be writing these anyway, but do note, that most of these optional forms are identical, and are used ionly in the even numbered cases.

Pay attention to only the singular forms for now. अहम् when used as a noun, understandably means, "Pride" in a negative sense. मम is another interesting word. Spiritually, it signifies desires, wishes, and possiveness. ममत्व or "mine-hood" is not a virtue. ममता is its feminine form indicating love or attachment.

Personal Pronouns, Plural:

यूयं वयं वयं यूयमित्यासिन्मतिरावयोः ।

→ यूयं वयं वयं यूयं इति आसित् मतिः आवयोः ।

यूयं = "You", first case plural form of
युष्मत् = "You".
त्वम्, युवाम्, यूयम्

आसित् = Was. From
अस् = To be
मति = Thinking, sense, attitude.

194

☞ Note the long "U" or "OO" in यूयम् as compared to युष्मद् and its other forms.

वयं = "We", first case plural form of
अस्मत् = "I".
अहम्, आवाम्, वयम्

आवयोः= "Our", sixth case plural

किं जातमधुना येन यूयं यूयं वयं वयम् ॥   →

येन = So that, literally, "by what", third case singular form of
यत् = "Which"
किम् = What
जात = Has happened. From
जन् (जा) = To be born.
अधुना = Now
आधुनिक = Modern.

"(Previously) 'You are us, and we are you' that was our thinking. Now what has happened, so that you are you, and we are we (without you)?"

Although sounding like a lament, it is actually said by a person who has seen his/her true self, and has achieved detachment. Our apparent unity is only an illusion created by our ignorant, and hence attached minds.

The Next Most Important Person —"You" :

The second person is the one we are talking to. (S)he is important, because (S)he may be our spouse, or at least someone who cares enough to listen to us - the most important person ! Let me show you its declension. Note the same things as we did with the first person.

युष्मद् ("You")

Case	Singular	Dual	Plural
१.	त्वम्	युवाम्	यूयम्
२.	त्वाम् (त्वा)	युवाम् (वाम्)	युष्मान् (नः)
३.	त्वया	युवाभ्याम्	युष्माभिः
४.	तुभ्यम् (ते)	युवाभ्याम् (वाम्)	युस्मभ्यम्
५.	त्वत्	युवाभ्याम्	युस्मत्
६.	तव (ते)	युवयोः (वाम्)	युस्माकम् (वः)
७.	त्वयि	युवयोः	युष्मासु

☞ Note that these are not any different from those of अस्मद्.

☞ नः for "Us", and वः for "You" may remind you of Spanish Nosotros and Vosotros.

☞ The first and the second person forms are gender neutral. They are used for masculine, feminine, and neuter genders alike.

त्वम् or "You" is extremely commonly used for the गुरु and for God. You will come across that in innumerable prayers.

त्वमेव माता च पिता त्वमेव
त्वमेव बंधुश्च सखा त्वमेव ।
त्वमेव विद्या द्रविणं त्वमेव
त्वमेव सर्वं मम देवदेव ॥

Only You are the mother, Only You are the father,
Only You are the brother, Only You are the friend;
Only You are the knowledge, Only You are the wealth,
Only You are my everything, O God of gods !

If the true knowledge is one that liberates us, then what more does one need to know about, than the Lord? With He being with us, what other wealth can we ask for?

तुभ्यम् (ते) should become familiar. When respect is being offered, the recepient takes the fourth case form. नमस्ते means, "I bow to you", and you have most likely heard that phrase many times.

ते is not used in the beginning of a sentence, but its place is taken by the optional form तुभ्यम् as in the following prayer. Its full discussion appears in the Treasure Chest later on.

तुभ्यं नमस्त्रिभुवनार्तिहराय नाथ !
तुभ्यं नमः क्षितितलामलभूषणाय ।
तुभ्यं नमस्त्रिजगतः परमेश्वराय
तुभ्यं नमो जिन ! भवोदधिशोषणाय ! ॥

I bow to you, the destroyer of darkness
from all three worlds, O Master !
I bow to you, O adornment of
the surface of this world;
I bow to you, O suprenme Lord
of the three worlds,
I bow to you, O conqurer of thy Self !
The great liberator !

We Have Company !
The Third Person "He/She/It":

This one is the real fun. It is the easiest one to simplify, because it is so complicated. With only one stone, we can kill all the remaining birds. It includes all pronouns, personal or otherwise, but let us finish the personal pronouns first.

The third person forms are gender sensitive, unlike the other two. Therefore, just as in English, we have to contend with three different declensions. Fortunately, they are not that dissimilar.

I will list the declensions for all three genders one after the other. Pay attention to their singular forms first. You will note that they resemble the declensions of राम, सीता, and वन representing the masculine, feminine, and the neuter genders respectively.

You may recall that declensions of वन were nearly identical to those of राम. The same is the case here. The neuter and the masculine pronouns have nearly identical declensions. just look at the following:

तद् *(Masculine, "He")*

Case	Singular	Dual	Plural
१.	सः	तौ	ते
२.	तम्	तौ	तान्
३.	तेन	ताभ्याम्	तैः
४.	तस्मै	ताभ्याम्	तेभ्यः
५.	तस्मात्	ताभ्याम्	तेभ्यः
६.	तस्य	तयोः	तेषाम्
७.	तस्मिन्	तयोः	तेषु

198

तद् *(Feminine, "She")*

Case	Singular	Dual	Plural
१.	*सा*	*ते*	*ताः*
२.	*ताम्*	*ते*	तान्
३.	*तया*	*ताभ्याम्*	*ताभिः*
४.	*तस्यै*	*ताभ्याम्*	*ताभ्यः*
५.	*तस्याः*	*ताभ्याम्*	*ताभ्यः*
६.	*तस्याः*	*तयोः*	*तासाम्*
७.	*तस्याम्*	*तयोः*	*तासु*

****

तद् *(Neuter, "It")*

Case	Singular	Dual	Plural
१.	*तद्*	*ते*	*तानि*
२.	*तद्*	*ते*	*तानि*

The rest are like the masculine form of the personal pronoun, which I have copied below.

	Singular	Dual	Plural
३.	*तेन*	*ताभ्याम्*	*तैः*
४.	*तस्मै*	*ताभ्याम्*	*तेभ्यः*
५.	*तस्मात्*	*ताभ्याम्*	*तेभ्यः*
६.	*तस्य*	*तयोः*	*तेषाम्*
७.	*तस्मिन्*	*तयोः*	*तेषु*

Pay close attention to all the forms that are in the *italic* face. You are most likely to come across them. You may want to keep all these book-marked for ready access.

List a few other pronouns. → This, That, What, Who, Which.

Do you know their Sanskrit equivalents? → एतद्, अदस्, किम्, यत्,
Why did I give only four equivalents, instead of five?

→ Because किम् is used for both, "Who" and "What".

Can you elaborate a little more? → किम् is used for men, women (Who), and for things (What).

Actually, all the four pronouns listed above are used for men, women, and things.

Which one of them is a personal pronoun? → None. Although they are all used in the third person, they do not stand for "He/She/It".

Now, as they say in jokes, I have a bad news, and a good news! First, the bad news. Since all these pronouns are used for all three genders, each of them have declensions for each of the three genders.

So, what's the good news? → These declensions are same as those we saw in case of तत् above. अदस् is an exception, but we will skip that altogether.

Why? → Because you are not supposed to have any bad news here!

भाषासु मुख्या मधुरा
दिव्या गीर्वाणभारती ।
तस्माद्धि काव्यं मधुरं　　→

तस्माद्धि=	तस्मात् + हि
TH(E) =	T + H
तस्मात् =	"from that", the fifth case singular form of
तत् =	"That"
हि =	An adverb for emphasis.

तस्मादपि सुभाषितम् ॥　　→　अपि = "But"

　　"Amongst all languages, the chief and sweet
　　is the divine "language of gods" (Sanskrit).
　　Of that, the literature is sweet,
　　and in that too, the beautiful is the Subhashit".

As you recall, nouns, pronouns, adjectives, and some participles कृदंताः when used as nouns or adjectives, all undergo declensions. When linked to one another, they maintain a correspondence with one another by following the same declensions. For example, The handsom, Ram, and He, will undergo the declensions as सुंदरः रामः and सः । We can see some examples of pronouns in use.

What does not undergo declensions?　　→　अव्यय. Promise, this question will not be repeated, ever !

यस्य नास्ति स्वयं प्रज्ञा
शास्त्रं तस्य करोति किम् ?

What case are यस्य, तस्य, (रामस्य) ?		→	Sixth case, singular
			यस्य = whose
			यत् = who, what
			तस्य = His / Her/Its
			तत् = That
What does	किम् mean?	→	किम् = "What"
What is	नास्ति ?	→	नास्ति = न + अस्ति
			Is not
	स्वयं	→	Native, innate, inherent. (an अव्यय)
			स्व = Self
	प्रज्ञा	→	प्र + ज्ञा= Intellect
			ज्ञा = to know
Recall,	न हि ज्ञानेन सदृशं पवित्रमिहविद्यते ।		
What is	शास्त्रं ?	→	शास्त्र = Scripture
Can you comprehend यस्य नास्ति.....?		→	Try, it is not difficult!

"What good would the scriptures do to someone who has no innate intelligence?"

What would a fool gain by reading the scriptures? There are two more lines to answer that question. The answer is also in the form of a question.

लोचनाभ्यां विहीनस्य	→	Devoid of eyes.
		लोचन = Eye
		लोचनाभ्याम् <u>Of</u> two eyes

विहीन = Deprived
o f
विहीनस्य that person's

दर्पणः किं करिष्यति ?　　→　दर्पण = a mirror
　　　　　　　　　　　　　　दर्प = pride

The word दर्पण for a mirror is quite interesting. How many times do we look into a mirror
to admire ourselves! The Sanskrit word for
"mirror" comes directly from "pride" or "vanity".
They don't call it "vanity mirror" for nothing! Even
to see our imaginary beauty, we need our eyes,
maybe mental eyes. Without that, the mirror would
be of no use.

The scriptures are like a mirror. They show
us ourselves, and make us reflect on that.　In this
श्लोक, there is a satire on those who follow
scriptures blindly.

　　　*"What good would the scriptures
do to someone who has no innate
intelligence? What good would a mirror
be to a blind man?"*

* *

TENSES:

करिष्यति may look somewhat unfamiliar. Or
maybe not, thanks to its -ति ending. Yes, it's in the
third person singular. However, we have seen
words like पश्यति, अस्ति, etc., but none with a half ष.
There is one, तुष्यति (He / She / It is satisfied), but
not many.

More often than not, this -इष्यति ending is a
hint that we are dealing with the future tense.

203

Don't let that make you tense at all. That's about all there is to it.

☞ -इष्यति indicates the future tense.

What about तुष्यति ? Well, it does indeed contain the ending -ष्यति, but not -इष्यति. As we saw with करिष्यति, our familiar endings -मि, -सि, -ति, -न्ति will still be there.

Unless you are getting tired, you will appreciate the fun, if I tell you that the संस्कृत word for the Future is भविष्य. You do remember भू (भव्) meaning, "to be". So, भविष्य is actually the future tense of भू (भव्).

When we looked at कृदंत, we saw गत (gone), हत (killed), etc. भूत means, "has been", that is, "it was". The past tense in संस्कृत is called भूत. भूत also means, "beings" or all creatures, and in a restricted sense, it means, "a spirit, or a ghost". This is really not that spooky. Great people or "Important Beings" are addressed as भवान् or "Your Majesty !"

Also, we saw हन्यमान् (one who is being hurt). There is a similar word वर्तमान् from वृत्, meaning, 'to happen". वर्तमानपत्र is "newspaper", (पत्र being "a leaf, or a sheet") and the name for the present tense is वर्तमान । To conclude this interesting digression, the word for Time is काळ.
Therefore,

The Present Tense	वर्तमान काळ
The Future Tense	भविष्य काळ
The Past Tense	भूत काळ

Write the future tense -ति forms of the following verbs:

गम् (गच्छ्)		→	गमिष्यति
भू (भव्)		→	भविष्यति
उद्	To rise	→	उदेष्यति
हस्	To laugh, smile	→	हसिष्यति

Try to understand and enjoy this:

रात्रिर्गमिष्यति भविष्यति सुप्रभातम् ।　→

रात्रि	=	Night
सु—	=	Good—
प्रभात	=	Dawn

भास्वानुदेष्यति हसिष्यति पंकजश्री ॥　→

भास्	=	Light
भास्वान्		the Sun
पंकज	=	a lotus, "mud-born"
श्री	=	affluence

You should have no problem with this lovely श्लोकार्ध, or half श्लोक.

*"The night shall go,
Good dawn will come;
the Sun will rise, (and)
Lotuses will blossom !"*

If the future tense was that easy, the past can't be difficult. Can you name at least two ways in which we can spot the past tense?

→	गत =	gone
→	गत्वा =	Having gone
→	निहत्य =	Having killed

All these are participles, or part-verbs. What about the complete verbs? One characteristic which marks the past tense verbs, is the उपसर्ग अ-.

For example:

पश्यति	He sees.
अपश्यत्	He saw.
अगच्छत्	He went.

Note that the -ति ending is lost. पश्यति becomes अपश्यत्, not अपश्यति । Actually, the verbs have special declensions for each of the three tenses, वर्तमान, भूत, and भविष्य काळाः ।

☞　　　Look at the ending to make sure you are actually looking at a verb, because अ- is also used as a negative prefix, or पूर्वग.

रसिक	Interested	अरसिक	→ Uninterested
प्रिय	Dear	अप्रिय	→ Unappealing
वास्तविक	Realistic	अवास्तविक	→ Unrealistic
स्पृश्य	Touchable	अस्पृश्य	→ "Untouchable", the lowest caste, शुद्र.

206

Let us continue:

मामकाः पांडवाश्चैव   →   मामकाः पांडवाः च एव

किमकुर्वत संजय ।   →   किम् अकुर्वत

संजय is the person to whom the question is being asked.

> *"My children, and the Pandavas (my brother Pandu's children), what did they do (अकुर्वत), O Sanjay !"*

The above is the उत्तरार्ध (the latter half) of the very first stanza of the श्रीमद्भगवद्गीता.

What will you call the first or the former half?

    →   पूर्वार्ध.

पूर्व = Before

In the above line, the blind king धृतराष्ट्र, father of कौरवाः, asks his friend and courtier संजय possessing the divine "tele" vision (tele = far), to describe to him what's happening on the battlefield. अकुर्वत is the plural form, as opposed to अकुर्वत् which is singular.

* *

Verbs, in addition to having numbers, persons, and tenses, also have voice (active and passive). We saw one example of the passive voice earlier:

प्रारभ्यते न खलु विघ्नभयेन नीचैः   →   *"The work is not even begun by the worst kind of people, being fearful of anticipated obstacles".*

Ordinarily, we would say, "they don't begin working". That would be active voice. "is not done by" is the passive form. It is good to be able to recognize it. When the object, rather than the subject is more important, this passive voice *is used (by us)*. When the subject (the doer) is important, *we use* the active voice.

I went.
I slept.
I ate.

All fruits, viz., bananas, mangoes, peaches, oranges, are available here!

They are ready to be picked (by anyone).

The top three are in the active voice, the last two are in the passive one.

* *

Like people, verbs get "moody" also. We are familiar with a command, or the Imperative mood. It includes requests also. Basically, someone else is being asked to do something.

Give me that!

विदितमविदितं वा
सर्वमेतत्क्षमस्व !   →   Forgive all that, please !

We saw कृदंताः being used to indicate duty, mission, desirable action, etc. Just to remind you,

कार्य	Mission, deed
कर्तव्य	Duty
करणीय	(something) worth doing

208

All of the above were derived from कृ, meaning "to do". Now, let us look at how verbs can be used for the same purpose. In the following, the mood is used to indicate advice.

सत्यं ब्रूयात् प्रियं ब्रूयात्	→	*"Speak the truth, speak the pleasant".* ब्रू = to speak प्रिय = Pleasant
न ब्रूयात्सत्यमप्रियम् ।	→	न ब्रूयात् सत्यम् अप्रियम् । *'Speak not (even) true but unpleasant"*
प्रियं च नानृतं ब्रूयात्	→	अनृतं = Non-truth सत्यमेव जयते नानृतम् । *"Even if pleasant, speak not a lie",*
एषः धर्मः सनातनः ॥	→	*"This is the fundamental duty ('eternal religion')".* एतद् = This एषः = first case singular

Now I will write the same without doing any विग्रह of संधि. Don't worry about the grammatical rules involved, nor about the meaning, which you already know. You are more likely to see the above श्लोकः written like this:

सत्यं ब्रूयात्प्रियं ब्रूयान्नब्रूयात्सत्यमप्रियम्
प्रियं च नानृतं ब्रूयादेषः धर्मः सनातनः ॥

If you've already had too much of all this, the next piece of advice applies to me. You are welcome to read it though !

अति सर्वत्र वर्जयेत् ।	→	*"Always avoid the extremes."*
		अति = Excess
		वर्ज् = to avoid, to give up

What is the meaning of वर्ज्य, वर्जितव्य, वर्जनीय ? →   Worth giving up

For a student of संस्कृत, cigarettes — made from even the best known Virginia वर्जीनीया tobacco — are always वर्जनीया !

What is	अत्र ?	→	Here
	तत्र	→	There
	सर्वत्र	→	Everywhere
	सर्व	→	All
	बहु	→	Many
	बहुवचन	→	Plural
	बहुधा	→	In many ways
			एकं सद्विप्राः बहुधा वदन्ति

Advice can be more direct:

सत्यं वद !	→	*"Speak the truth"!*
धर्मं चर !	→	*"Practice the religion" !*
		"Do your duties"!
प्रसीद !	→	*"Be pleased !"*
		"Please"!
शुभं भवतु !	→	*"May good happen"!*
		"God bless you"!
तेजस्विनावधीतमस्तु !	→	तेजस्वि = Bright
		नौ = Our
		अधीतम् Intelligence
		अस्तु = Be
		"May we get smarter"!

There is an interesting संधि here that you are not familiar with. This one also takes place automatically, without any effort on your part.

नौ	+	अधीतम्		
औ	+	अ	=	आव् + अ = आव

नाव्	+	अधीतम्	=	नावधीतम्

HO	+	UR	=	"OUR" (HOUR)
ओ	+	अ	=	अव्

Thus, verbs can be used in various tenses, Moods, such as an order, as a benediction, or blessing, or as advice or an admonition. And of course, as part-verbs, or participles, कृदंत can be used in various other ways.

* *

Prepositions / Seventh case:

They are called Prepositions, because they are positioned before ("Pre-") a noun. However, that is not always the case in Sanskrit. They may follow a noun also. Unlike पूर्वगाः they are not literally attached to the noun.

करागे वसते लक्ष्मी	→	कर + अग्रे		
		कर	=	hand, from
		कृ	=	to do
		अग्र	=	front
करमूले सरस्वती ।	→	मूल	=	Root
करमध्ये तु गोविंदः	→	मध्य	=	Middle
प्रभाते करदर्शनम् ॥	→	प्रभात	=	dawn
		दर्शन	=	to see

211

In the above, I am sure you had no difficulty in recognizing the seventh case forms,

अग्रे	At the tip of
मूले	At the base of
मध्ये	In the middle
प्रभाते	At the daybreak.

The last one indicates the time, and hence it is in the seventh case. The first three indicate the place, and therefore, are also in the seventh case. They differ from the last one in a small, but easily noticeable way. They show the relationship between two nouns, and therefore, in English, they will be considered to be Prepositions:

Hand	At its tip	Laxmi, the goddess of wealth
Hand	At its base	Saraswati, the goddess of Learning
Hand	In its middle.	
	In the palm	Govind, that is, Lord Krishna.

"*The godess of wealth resides at the tip of the hand,*
that of knowledge lives at its root,
the Lord Krishna Himself lives in the palm,
(therefore) one should look at the palm first thing in the morning."

The above is not to be taken literally. Dawn is the early state of enlightenment. Hand symbolizes action or deeds. Any action that is rooted in true knowledge, and has the Lord right in the middle of it, always leads to fruition.

☞   Poetry is subjective. Hence, many of the Sanskrit श्लोकाः and सुभाषितानि are open to several interpretations, all of them being correct in their way.

       Without memorizing, just notice that the seventh case indicates the time and place relationship between nouns and verbs. On the other hand, the Prepositions indicate the relationship between two nouns.

☞   In Sanskrit, there is actually nothing that is exactly the same as Prepositions. Seventh case forms of nouns or adjectives are used for that purpose.

☞   Prepositions are supposed to be अव्यय, but the seventh - or any other - case forms by definition, are not अव्यय.

☞   In Gujarati and other languages derived from Sanskrit, there are Prepositions. They are called नामयोगी अव्यय (noun-uniting, unchanging words). By definition, they are not supposed to have any case-forms.

Conjunctions and Interjections:

       We saw many examples of these. Just to refresh your memory, I listed a few of them below:

Conjunctions: च, अपि, वा, तथा.
Interjections: हे! भो! धिक्!, रे!.

With this, you have successfully completed your study of very basic संस्कृत, enough to enable you to appreciate and enjoy the beauty and charm of this divine language. I would like to compliment you on your perseverance.

Understandably, what you went through was not easy, but let me assure you, I simplified it several hundred times! Even when having fun, there is some price to pay. However, the price should not amount to torture!

I don't mean to imply, that study of संस्कृत is torture, even when it is done in an orthodox way. I myself studied like that, and all I can recall is fond memories. So, if you enjoyed what you just finished, you should pursue a formal study of संस्कृत now, without any apprehension !

Your Indian temple priest may provide some coaching, or may guide you further. Learn to pronounce the संस्कृत words clearly and correctly. शुद्धि or purity is very important in prayers, in chanting, and for appreciating the real lyrical beauty of various hymns and सुभाषितानि । Do not even for a moment, get the wrong idea that संस्कृत is all prayers and advice only. Far from it.

There are innumerable excellent stories, poems, and plays in it. The great epics रामायण, and महाभारत are in संस्कृत. रामायण is the story of Lord राम and of his conquering the demon रावण, who had abducted रामस्य wife सीता ।

महाभारत is the story woven around the 18-day battle between first cousins — one hundred supposedly wicked कौरवाः and five all too human पांडवाः । Lord कृष्ण, an incarnation, like राम, of Lord विष्णु, is also a major character in this epic.

श्रीमद्भगवद्गीता is integral, and although very small, the most important part of महाभारत. It is a dialogue between Lord कृष्ण, and his friend and disciple अर्जुन. Arjun, the second oldest पांडव prince was overcome with despondency, when he realized that he had to kill many of his own relatives to achieve victory and win justice. This booklet, loaded with सुभाषितानि, is the heart of Hindu philosophy, and is the science of life.

श्रीमद्भागवतम् (श्रीमद् भागवतम्) is like the Old Testament of the Holy Bible, and is full of interesting stories. It delineates all (ten of which were major) incarnations of the Lord विष्णु. It also deals with the Creation, but in a metaphorical way.

I did mention earlier कालिदास, who wrote the excellent play अभिज्ञान शाकुंतलम् ("Identification of the woman named शकुंतला"), the famous poem रघुवंश, about राम and his dynasty, the lyrical मेघदूत, wherein a separated celestial lover sends to his beloved, a message to be carried by a rain cloud acting as a messanger. It is full of शृंगार (which can be badly translated as "sex"). His third well known poem कुमारसंभव is a masterpiece in its depiction of शृंगार of the holy couple शंकर and पार्वती.

There are many universities, those of Pennsylvania and of Chicago, in the U.S.A., and many more in the U.K. and in Germany, not to mention in India, from where many excellent संस्कृत works including the वेदाः, उपनिषदाः, स्मृतयः, श्रुतयः, पुराणाः ("ancient" books), etc., with their English translations and commentaries are available.

The University of Chicago's पंचतंत्र (Stories in "Five Sections") is a notable collection of stories which are full of worldly wisdom and advice for achieving success.

I would advise you to get the English, or one of the Indian language translations, with the original संस्कृत text included. The latter is very important. You may not read or understand all the संस्कृत text on your own. Just try to read it, then read the meaning, and then go back to the original.

Invariably, you will find the original far more interesting. Translations are mere approximations. You may recall the संस्कृत word for Fantasy — मनोरथ or "chariot of mind !" संस्कृत words शृंगार, मंगल ("holy"), etc. are far more expressive than their English counterparts. For fairness, I should admit that I have yet to see a good Indian language translation of such simple lament as, "To be, or not to be..."

One warning! From now on, do not read the English transliteration of any संस्कृत writing. Now you know very well how to read and enjoy the original संस्कृत writings.

Once again, congratulations !

....

PART : IV
THE TREASURE CHEST

....

I won't try to guess whether you will be disappointed or delighted to hear that in this part, there will be no formal teaching. This is not a driving test, with the inspector judging your every action. Instead, think of this as taking a new car for a test drive, with an eager and enthusiastic sales person pointing out the beauty of the car and its stereo system at every opportunity.

This is real life Sanskrit. Again, relax. Yes, it is a test, but that of the car, not of you. You just enjoy the ride. Read the original first, on your own. Don't skip this crucial part. You are not expected to be able to understand everything. Just look for anything that you can recognize, be it a noun, a pronoun, a verb conjugation, a case, a number, the sign of deletion, and per chance, the complete meaning of a word. Bravo, miracles do happen, and we are dealing with the divine language!

Dwell on the original, savor its sound, its rhythm, its nasal softness, its harsh diphthongs or joined letters, its short or long meter, the way it looks, etc. Remember, you don't have to know anything about the wavelength of light, or its spectral analysis, to enjoy a lovely sunrise or sunset. Knowing that may even decrease the pleasure. Compliment yourself on whatever you can appreciate on your own.

Continue to put the worries about the car's horse power, engine torque, and the drive train warranty out of your mind. Don't plunge into learning mode either. With fun in mind, and nothing else, read the translation, intentionally kept literal to enhance your appreciation. You may want to think about the charm of the words in front of you, and how warmly they greet you !

षड् दोषाः पुरुषेणेह
हातव्या भूतिमिच्छता ।
निद्रा तंद्रा भयं क्रोधः
आलस्यं दीर्घसूत्रता ॥

These six shortcomings should be avoided by any man
Desiring wealth in this world:
Sleep, inattention, fear, anger,
Laziness, and procrastination.

*   *   *   *   *   *   *   *   *   *   *   *

शोकस्थान सहस्राणि
भयस्थान शतानि च ।
दिवसे दिवसे मूढम्
आविशन्ति न पंडितम् ॥

Thousands of things to grieve about,
And hundreds of things to be afraid of,
Day after day, to a dimwit,
(They) come, but not to a wise person.

*   *   *   *   *   *   *   *   *   *   *   *

मातृवत् परदारेषु
परद्रव्येषु लोष्टवत् ।
आत्मवत् सर्वभूतेषु
यः पश्यति सः पश्यति ॥

At someone's wife as his own mother,
At another's wealth as scrap iron,
In all living beings as himself,
(The man) who looks Is the one who (really) sees !
                    (all others are blind)

*   *   *   *   *   *   *   *   *   *   *   *

येषां न विद्या न तपो न दानं
ज्ञानं न शीलं न गुणो न धर्मः ।
ते मृत्युलोके भुविभारभूता
मनुष्यरूपेण मृगाश्चरन्ति ॥ (नीतिशतक)

(Talking) of those with no skills, no austerities, no charities,
No knowledge, no character, no virtue, no sense of duty;
They are a burden on this earth,
Wandering animals (disguised) in the human form.

धर्म :   *This is generally translated as "religion", but it carries a very complex meaning which needs to be appreciated.* धर्म *also means one's duty. This duty may be born out of one's past or out of contracts, promises, etc.* धर्म *also means "righteousness".*

The most important is, it may be exactly the opposite of conventional religion. One may be a follower of a religion advocating extreme non-violence. (S)he may find him/her in a situation, in which killing someone instantly may be the only way to save hundreds or thousands of lives.

Does the religion now approve of violence? No. Does saving many lives permit one to do wrong? No. These are the decisions that the person himself or herself has to make. (S)he has to decide what is the धर्म *in that situation. All these, and more are implied by the word* धर्म.

After considering and weighing everything, what is "incumbent upon us" is our धर्म !

*   *   *   *   *   *   *   *   *   *   *   *

विद्या नाम नरस्य रूपमधिकं प्रच्छन्नगुप्तं धनम्
विद्या भोगकरी यशःसुखकरी विद्या गुरुणां गुरुः ।
विद्या बन्धुजनो विदेशगमने विद्या परा देवता
विद्या राजषु पूजिता न तु धनं विद्याविहीनः पशुः ॥ (नीतिशतक)

(An asset named) Knowledge is a man's unique beauty,
a secretly hidden treasure.
Knowledge creates comforts, prestige, and pleasures.
Knowledge is the teacher of teachers.
Knowledge is the brother (friend) away from the home land,
Knowledge is the supreme deity.
Knowledge is honored at the (king's) court, and not wealth.
(The one) without Knowledge, is a beast !

* * * * * * * * * * * *

ऐश्वर्यस्य विभूषणं सुजनता शौर्यस्य वाक्संयमो
ज्ञानस्योपशमः श्रुतस्य विनयो वित्तस्य पात्रे व्ययः ।
अक्रोधस्तपसः क्षमा प्रभवितुर्धर्मस्य निर्व्याजिता
सर्वेषामपि सर्वकारणमिदं शीलं परं भूषणम् ॥   (नीतिशतक)

The adoration of riches is, being mild-mannered;
of bravery is control over the tongue,
Of knowledge is control of sense organs, of learning is modesty,
of wealth is spending for a worthy cause,
Of spiritual loftiness is lack of anger, of power is forgiveness,
of righteousness is absence of hypocrisy,
But of all of these, and for all reasons,
the best adoration is good character.

* * * * * * * * * * * *

न सा सभा यत्र न सन्ति वृद्धा
वृद्धा न ते ये न वदन्ति धर्मम् ।
धर्मो न वै यत्र च नास्ति सत्यं
सत्यं न तद्यच्छलनाऽनुविद्धम् ॥   (सत्यं न तत् यत् छलना अनुविद्धम्)

That is not a real assembly, where there are no old men.
They are not real old men, who do not speak the Dharm;
That is not the real Dharm though, where there is no truth.
That is not the truth, which does not exclude deception.

सुलभाः पुरुषाः लोके
सततं प्रियवादिनः ।
अप्रियस्यापि पथ्यस्य
वक्ता श्रोता च दुर्लभः ॥

Easily found are the men in this world
Who always talk sweet
Of the unpleasant, but the appropriate
Speakers and listeners are difficult to come by.

* * * * * * * * * * * *

जाड्यं धियो हरति सिंचति वाचि सत्यं
मानोन्नतिं दिशति पापमपाकरोति ।
चेतः प्रसादयति दिक्षु तनोति कीर्तिम्
सत्संगतिः कथय किं न करोति पुंसाम् ॥   (नीतिशतक)

(It) removes the sloth off the reason, pours truth into the speech,
shows a rise in one's respect, washes away sins,
pleases the sensorium, spreads one's fame far and wide,
what the contact with the good guys doesn't do for people, tell me !

* * * * * * * * * * * *

नास्ति कामसमो व्याधिः
नास्ति मोहसमो रिपुः ।
नास्ति क्रोधसमो वह्निः
नास्ति ज्ञानात्परं सुखम् ॥

There is no (other) disease like desire,
There is no enemy like attachment;
There is no fire like anger,
There is no better happiness than knowledge.

* * * * * * * * * * * *

अज्ञानतिमिरांधानां
ज्ञानांजनशलाक्या ।
चक्षुरुन्मीलितं येन
तस्मै श्री गुरवे नमः ॥

Blinded by the darkness of ignorance,
By instilling the ointment of knowledge,
(Our) eyes were opened by whom,
To that revered Guru, I bow down !

*   *   *   *   *   *   *   *   *   *   *   *

गुरुर्ब्रह्मा गुरुर्विष्णु-
र्गुरुर्देवो महेश्वरः ।
गुरु साक्षात्परब्रह्म
तस्मै श्री गुरवे नमः ॥

Guru is Brahma (the Creator), Guru is Lord Vishnu,
Guru is the great god (Shankar)
Guru is the incarnate supreme Absolute
To that revered Guru, I bow down !

ब्रह्म : *This is the supreme, absolute, cosmic element called God. On the other hand,* ब्रह्मा *is one of his His three aspects — the Creator.* विष्णु *is the Operating Manager, and* शंकर *is the Director of the Demolition Department, to clean up and ready the world for a new beginning.*

ब्रह्मा *is, understandably, the father of the goddess of learning,* सरस्वती. *And* विष्णु *is neccessarily, the master (husband) of the goddess of wealth* लक्ष्मी. शंकर *is married to the energy or* शक्ति. *She is the daughter of the great mountain or* पर्वत *that is the Himalaya* हिमालय, *and is known as* पार्वती.

For those who are still half-jokingly debating whether God is a man or a woman, here is the answer. शंकर *and* पार्वती *together form only one body, and hence is (not "are") called* अर्धनारीनरेश्वर *(half-woman-man-god)* !

222

पिबन्ति नद्यः स्वयमेव नाम्भः
स्वयं न खादन्ति फलानि वृक्षाः ।
धाराधरो वर्षति नात्महेतोः
परोपकाराय सतां विभूतयः ॥

Rivers themselves don't drink water,
Trees themselves don't eat fruits,
Clouds don't rain for themselves,
The riches of the good are for helping others !

* * * * * * * * * * * *

धैर्यं यस्य पिता क्षमा च जननी शांतिश्चिरं गेहिनी
सत्यं सूनुरयं दया च भगिनी भ्राता मनः संयमः ।
शय्या भूमितलं दिशोऽपि वसनं ज्ञानामृतं भोजनम्
एते यस्य कुटुम्बिनो वद सखे कस्माद्भयं योगिनः ॥

Patience is whose father, forgiveness mother, lasting peace wife,
Truth is son, mercy sister, self control brother,
Bare floor is the bed, sky is apparel, elixir of knowledge is dinner,
These are whose family, tell me friend, what such *Yogi* would fear !

योगी :   From युज् "to be united", practioner of Yoga
         योग, in search of Him.

दिशोऽपि वसनम् :   With no possessions, not even a cloth to
         cover the body. All directions दिशा (the sky)
         is their clothing वसनम्

* * * * * * * * * * * *

श्रुतिर्विभिन्ना स्मृतयश्च भिन्ना
नैको मुनिर्यस्य वचः प्रमाणम् ।
धर्मस्य तत्त्वं निहितं गुहायाम्
महाजनो येन गतः सः पंथाः ॥

The Shrities don't agree, the Smrities are not unanimous,
There is no one authority, whose word to go by,
The nucleus of the Truth (Dharma) is hidden in caves,
Travelled by the great ones, are the paths (to follow).

श्रुति : Scriptures re-written by listening to the seniors.

स्मृति : Scriptures re-written from memory.

मुनि : The ones who really know, generally keep quiet or मौन,
and are called मुनि. There are many such experts, who
give differing opinions.

*   *   *   *   *   *   *   *   *   *   *   *

वज्रादपि कठोराणि मृदुनि कुसुमादपि ।
लोकोत्तराणां चेतांसि को हि विज्ञातुमर्हति ॥

Harder than the lightning bolt, (yet) softer than flowers,
(Such) minds of super-human (people), only some can understand !

वज्र :   The lightening bolt wielded by ईन्द्र the rain god. ईन्द्र
is the Indian counterpart of Zeus or Jupiter of the
Greeks and the Romans. But he is a minor god,
unlike that of Homer. Since the lightning bolt can
crack open even the mountains, it is considered to
be very hard.

लोकोत्तर: लोक = "where the life is". There are three लोकाः, the
heavens, the hell, and the middle one filled with us
mortals, called मर्त्य लोक (Mortal), or the मध्य लोक
(middle). उत्तर means "beyond", and लोकोत्तर or लोक
उत्तर is "Out of This World", super-human people
like Mahatma Gandhi, whom not all of us can
comprehend.

*   *   *   *   *   *   *   *   *   *   *   *

निन्दन्तु नीतिनिपुणाः यदि वा स्तुवन्तु
लक्ष्मीः समाविशतु गच्छतु वा यथेष्टम् ।
अद्यैव वा मरणमस्तु युगान्तरे वा
न्यायात्पथः प्रविचलन्ति पदं न धीराः ॥   (नीतिशतक)

Whether the politicians criticize, or praise (them),
The wealth may come or go as it wishes,
The death may come now, or after the ages,
The steadfast ones don't stray even one step
                    from the path of justice.

*   *   *   *   *   *   *   *   *   *   *   *

वांछा सज्जनसंगमे परगुणे प्रीतिर्गुरौ नम्रता
विद्यायां व्यसनं स्वयोषिति रतिर्लोकापवादाद्भयम् ।
भक्तिश्चक्रिणि शक्तिरात्मदमने संसर्गमुक्ति खले
एते यत्र वसन्ति निर्मलगुणास्तेभ्यो नरेभ्यो नमः ॥   (नीतिशतक)

Desire for good company, love for others' virtues,
                    humility in front of seniors,
Affinity for knowledge, pleasure in one's wife,
                    fear of public censure,
Devotion to Lord Vishnu, striving for self control,
                    avoiding bad company,
In whom such pure virtues reside,
                    I bow to that man !

*   *   *   *   *   *   *   *   *   *   *   *

धृष्टं धृष्टं पुनरपि पुनश्चंदनं चारुगंधं
छिन्नं छिन्नं पुनरपि पुनः स्वादु चैवेक्षुकांडम् ।
दग्धं दग्धं पुनरपि पुनः कांचनं कांतवर्णम्
प्राणांतेऽपि प्रकृतिविकृतिर्जयते नोत्तमानाम् ॥

Crushed, crushed again and again sandlewood becomes fragrant,
Cut, cut, again and again, a piece of sugar-cane becomes tasty,
Burnt, burnt, again and again, gold becomes glittering,
Even at the time of death, the great ones' nature doesn't change !

225

मूलं भुजंगैः शिखरं प्लवंगैः
शाखा विहंगैः कुसुमानि भृंगैः ।
आसेव्यते दुष्टजनैः समस्तैः
न चंदनं मुंचति शीतलत्वम् ॥

The root by snakes, the top by monkeys,
The branches by birds (smearing it), the flowers by wasps,
(Even though) surrounded by bad guys in every which way,
The sandlewood (tree) does not give up its cool (nature) !

*   *   *   *   *   *   *   *   *   *   *   *

सा विद्या या विमुक्तये !

That is the real knowledge, which liberates ! (Know thy self!)

*   *   *   *   *   *   *   *   *   *   *   *

शिवास्ते पंथानः सन्तु !

May your paths bring good to you ! (Bon voyage !)

*   *   *   *   *   *   *   *   *   *   *   *

शतं जीव शरदः !

May you live a hundred years !

शरद :   The later half of the Monsoon is called
शरद, and is the unhealthiest season.

*   *   *   *   *   *   *   *   *   *   *   *

मातृ देवो भव !
पितृ देवो भव !
आचार्य देवो भव !
अतिथि देवो भव !

The mother is God !
The father is God !
The teacher is God !
The guest is God !

(Yes, the guest is God, too! You never know
when He will appear at your door!)

*   *   *   *   *   *   *   *   *   *   *   *

क्षणे क्षणे यन्नवतामुपैति   (यत् नवताम् उपैति)
तदेव रूपं रमणीयतायाः ।

(At) every moment, which achieves novelty,
That is what the *beauty* is !

रमणीयता :   From रम् *("to please"),* रमणी *is one of the hundreds
of synonyms for "a woman". Although the word*
रमणीयता *is also used for other kinds of beauties, it
generally refers to feminine beauty.*

*   *   *   *   *   *   *   *   *   *   *   *

मुक्ताफलेषु छायायाः तरलत्वमिवान्तराः ।
प्रतिभाति यदंगेषु तल्लावण्यमिहोच्यते ॥

Like the fickleness of reflections in a pearl,
What glows from the body, is called Beauty (L<u>a</u>vanya) !

लावण्य :   *You simply cannot ignore the similarity with what
we call "Lovely"! It refers to youthful beauty.
"Lovely" doesn't do as much justice to beauty, as*
लावण्य *does.*

*   *   *   *   *   *   *   *   *   *   *   *

227

वैकल्पीय भारतीय राष्ट्रगीत
कवि : श्री. बंकीमचन्द्र चट्टोपाध्याय

The Alternate Indian National Anthum
Poet : Mr. Bankimchandra Chattopadhyay.

वंदे मातरम् । वंदे मातरम् ।

सुजलाम् सुफलाम्
मलयज शीतलाम्
सस्यश्यामलाम्
मातरम्, वंदे मातरम्   ॥ १. ॥

शुभ्रज्योत्स्ना-पुलकित-यामिनीम्
फुल्ल-कुसुमिता-द्रुम-दल-शोभिनीम्
सुहासिनीम् सुमधुरभाषिनीम्
सुखदाम् वरदाम्, मातरम्, वंदे मातरम्   ॥ २. ॥

I bow to the Mother (India), I bow to the Mother !

To the one with good waters, good fruits,
To the Malay-mountain-(wind)-cooled,
To the one with blue green farms,
To the Mother, I bow to the Mother !   (1.)

To the one with white-moonlit-pleasant-nights,
To the blossoming-flowers-studded-forests-adorned,
To the one with good smile, especially sweet speech,
To the pleasures-giver, blessings-giver,
To the Mother, I bow to the Mother !   (2.)

*   *   *   *   *   *   *   *   *   *   *   *

प्रार्थनाः PRAYERS

विद्यामंदिरस्य प्रार्थना

ॐ सहनाववतु ।
सह नौ भुनक्तु ।
सह वीर्यं करवावहै ।
तेजस्वीनावधीतमस्तु ।
मा विद्विषावहै ।
ॐ शांतिः शांतिः शांतिः ।

The School (Temple of Learning) Prayer:

Om! May He protect both of us (गुरु and शिष्य)
May he employ both of us (in His missions)
May we strive together.
May our intellect brighten.
May we not despise each other.
Om! Peace (be here), peace (be there), peace (be everywhere) !

ॐ :   *This is not a letter of the Devanagari alphabet, but
is a symbol, like the Swastika, with similar spiritual
significance. The three prongs of the part which looks
like "3" signify three worlds, the tail is the path away
from there, and the dot above the crescent is the
ultimate salvation. This is a pictographic symbol of the
entire Hindu philosophy. The symbol is read as deep
"O.....m !"*

*   *   *   *   *   *   *   *   *   *   *   *

असतो मा सद्गमय !
तमसो मा ज्योतिर्गमय !
मृत्योर्मा अमृतं गमय !

From the un-truth, to the Truth, take me Thou !
From the deep dark, to the Light, take me Thou !
From the great death, to near immortality, take me Thou !

यं ब्रह्मा वरुणेन्द्र रुद्र मरुतः स्तुन्वन्ति दिव्यैस्तवैः
वेदैः सांगपदक्रमोपनिषदैः गायन्ति यं सामगाः ।
ध्यानावस्थित तद्गतेन मनसा पश्यन्ति यं योगिनो
यस्यान्तं न विदुः सुरासुरगणाः देवाय तस्मै नमः ॥

Whom Brahma, Rudra, Wind-god praise with divine songs,
Whom the singers of the Samved praise with the Vedas, etc.
Whom the Yogis, by focusing their mind in Him, can see,
Whose end, gods and others cannot perceive, to that God, I bow !

*(This stanza offers prayer to the One
Supreme being. Hinduism is somewhat erroneously
labelled as a religion with many gods, i.e., it is
poly-theistic. This prayer makes it clear that all
other deities are nothing but the aspects of the One
Highest being.)*

*   *   *   *   *   *   *   *   *   *   *   *

वक्रतुंड ! महाकाय !
सूर्यकोटिसमप्रभ !
निर्विघ्नं कुरु मे देव !
शुभ कार्येषु सर्वदा !

O, the Round Bellied (Lord Ganesha) ! O, the Big bodied !
O, with the radiance like that of ten million Suns !
Make it a trouble free zone, O god !
In all my good works, always !

*   *   *   *   *   *   *   *   *   *   *   *

या कुंदेन्दु तुषारहार धवला या शुभ्रवस्त्रावृता
या वीणावरदंडमंडितकरा ! या श्वेतपद्मासना !
या ब्रह्माच्युतशंकरप्रभृतिभिः देवैः सदा वंदिता
सा मां पातु सरस्वती भगवती निःशेष जाड्यापहा ॥

Who is pure white like the Moon, the dew, and Kund flowers,
              who is wrapped in a white fabric,
who is with the string-Veena's-lovely-shaft-holding-hands,
              who is seated on a white lotus flower;
Who is, by Brahma, Vishnu, Shankar, and all other gods,
              has always been honored,
May that revered goddess Saraswati save me, and
              Destroy all the sloth from my mind !

(सरस्वती is the goddess of learning. She is pure, and is an eternal virgin, and yet, is called "mother". Everything about her is white. There are three synonyms of "white" here, viz., धवल, शुभ्र, and श्वेत. She carries a string instrument in her hand, and if you say the first part of the second line या वीणा...... out loud, you can even hear it.)

*   *   *   *   *   *   *   *   *   *   *   *

तुभ्यं नमस्त्रिभुवनार्तिहराय नाथ !
तुभ्यं नमः क्षितितलामलभूषणाय ।
तुभ्यं नमस्त्रिजगतः परमेश्वराय
तुभ्यं नमो जिन ! भवोदधिशोषणाय ! ॥   (श्री. भक्तामर स्तोत्र)

I bow to you, the destroyer of darkness
              from all three worlds, O Master !
I bow to you, O adornment of the surface of this world;
I bow to you, O suprenme Lord of the three worlds,
I bow to you, O conqueror of thy Self ! The great liberator !

The last part, "the great liberator", is a paraphrase. This is a Jain जैन prayer. Jains follow the Jinas जिनाः or "Conquerors" (जि = to conquer) of their Selves. The Jain / Budhdhist/ Hindu philosophy considers the soul's wandering from birth to birth as suffering. The journey through these births, innumerable ones, is compared to swimming an ocean. Jina's mercy is able, as if, to dry up this vast ocean. The last part literally says, "O dryer of the ocean of births and deaths !

231

शांताकारं भुजगशयनं पद्मनाभं सुरेशम्
विश्वाधारं गगनसदृशं मेघवर्णं शुभांगम् ।
लक्ष्मीकांतं कमलनयनं योगिभिः ध्यानगम्यम्
वंदे विष्णुं भवभयहरं सर्वलोकैकनाथम् ॥

To the one with a peaceful disposition, with snake as his bed,
        with a lotus sprouting from the belly button, God of gods,
To the support of the world, vast like the sky,
        Rain-cloud-hued, beautiful-bodied;
To the master (husband) of goddess Laxmi, lotus-like-eyed,
        Accessible by the meditating Yogis,
I bow to Lord Vishnu ! Remover of the fear of cycles of birth,
        the One and the Only Master of all the three worlds !

Monotheistic abstract God becomes more accessible to our simple minds by way of His aspects. One can reach the same Lord by way of any of the aspects. There are many श्लोकाः and प्रार्थनाः describing this or that aspect of the cosmic ॐ, or ब्रह्म are only superficially contradictory.

Lord Vishnu lives at the bottom of the ocean, relaxing on top of the coiled snake शेषनाग (whose stirrings supposedly cause earthquakes), with the Wealth (that is, "Earth", source of all wealth), massaging His feet. From His belly button, sprouts a lotus, in which ब्रह्म the creator aspect materializes and does the Creation. These are all metaphors presented in delightful poetry. Description of each of the Lord's attributes provides an interesting contrast from the next juxtaposed segment.

*   *   *   *   *   *   *   *   *   *   *   *

मूकं करोति वाचालं पंगुं लंघयते गिरिम् ।
यत्कृपा तमहं वंदे परमानंद माधवम् ॥

Makes the mute vocal, and enables the lame to climb a mountain,
Whose mercy, to Him I bow down, the supreme bliss, Krishna !

232

Lord Vishnu, whose incarnations include राम *and* कृष्ण, *goes by more than a thousand descriptive names.* माधव, मुरारि, हरि, केशव, अच्यूत, लक्ष्मीकांत, पद्मनाभ, मुकुंद *(see the next prayer), are only a few examples. In addition to several other benefits, this abundance of names allows poets to work one of these names into a given meter. However, it is not that simple. The* संस्कृत *poets generally, and amazingly, have managed to use the most appropriate name in each instance, irrespective of poetic considerations.*

*   *   *   *   *   *   *   *   *   *   *   *

करारविंदेन पदारविंदं
मुखारविंदे विनिवेशयन्तम् ।
वटस्य पत्रस्य पुटे शयानं
बालं मुकुंदं मनसा स्मरामि ॥

By the lotus-like hand, (holding) the lotus-like foot,
Inserting it into the lotus-like mouth;
Lying on a pile of Banyan tree leaves,
The Baby Krishna, I visualize in my mind.

This is a simple and delightful depiction of Krishna, the child. Just see the simple elegance of a child's description. Lying down playfully on a pile of leaves, grabbing his foot with his hand, and trying to put it into his mouth. That's the universal description of an infant. कृष्ण *grew up in the ruling family of a town of cowherds.*

*   *   *   *   *   *   *   *   *   *   *   *

समुद्रवसने देवि !
पर्वतस्तनमंडले !
विष्णुपत्नी नमस्तुभ्यं
पादस्पर्शं क्षमस्व मे !

O, the ocean-clad goddess !
O, the one with mountains as the breasts !
O, the wife of Lord Vishnu ! I bow to you,
Forgive me for touching you with my feet !

This is a prayer of Laxmi, the goddess of wealth, that is none other than the Earth. Thousands of years before airplanes and helicopters were invented, this poet could imagine the Earth as a woman, wearing the blue oceans as her Sari wrapped around her. This mother of all abundance, can have nothing less than the mountains as her breasts. All respects go to her. However, how can we touch her with our feet?

IMMEASURABLE PLEASURE

The सुभाषितानि we have seen thus far were beautiful and full of wisdom, spiritual as well as worldly. I pointed out their beauty in a very general way. I hope you were able to appreciate the union of various consonants and vowels (संधि), and of two or more words (समास).

समासाः are very interesting, but you may not share my enthusiasm, so we'll leave their detailed elaboration out. Suffice it to say that not all समासाः are alike, and their component words may be mutually related in many different manners.

The ancient Sanskrit literature is mostly in poetry (पद्य), with many excellent stories, plays, etc. in prose (गद्य). Even the latter contain many stanzas of poems. Ancient poems were and are very lyrical, and it is a delight to sing them out loud. They employ several different meters, depending upon the mood, tempo, feelings (भाव), and how the latter are perceived (रस meaning, "a taste"). There are nine रसाः, viz., comic or हास्य, tragic or करुण, romantic/sensual or श्रृंगार, tranquil or शांत, disgusting (full of blood and gore) or बीभत्स, and so on. You may want to appreciate these while reading any Sanskrit work.

The beauty of the human body depends upon good proportions, or stated crudely, upon the "measurements". And it is enhanced by the judicious use of ornaments. The same is true for poetry, at least the ancient one. I will let you in on its secrets, to enhance your enjoyment greatly, with very little effort on your part. In poetry, these two —measurements and ornaments — are known as Meters and Figures of Speech, or छंद and अलंकार ("ornament") respectively.

METERS छंदाः

We will not go into the kind of meters wherein each line of a stanza carries a specific number of short and long sounds in any combination (मात्रावृत्ताः). We will limit ourselves to those meters (अक्षरवृत्ताः), which contain a *fixed number* of short and long syllables (अक्षराः) arranged in a *fixed sequence*. As illustrations, I have chosen श्लोकाः that go beyond piety, devotion, and wisdom, into other रसाः.

What follows is really nothing more than what common sense will tell you. As you know, any sound or syllable is either a short one, or a long one. अ, इ, उ, and ऋ, are the only short sounds, while the rest are long sounds.

All consonants with a nasal dot on top, and those with a विसर्ग are also long sounds. As you may recall, the accent is always on the letter preceding the conjoined consonants. Therefore, that letter is considered a long one. e.g., भक्त, कृष्ण, वर्तमान, because their syllables are Bhak-ta, Krish-na, and Var-ta-ma-n, respectively.

Short Sounds: अ, इ, उ, ऋ.

Long Sounds: आ, ई, ऊ, ए, ऐ, ओ, औ, (there is a long ऋ also).
Letters with a nasal dot on top, e.g., हंत, हन्त.
Letters with a विसर्ग, e.g., कः, सः
Letters before conjoined consonants, e.g., भक्त.
The last अक्षर of a line can be considered to be a long one, even if it is short.

You may also remember (thankfully, against my advice) that the word for "Short" is लघु, and that for the "Long" is गुरु. For simplicity, and to make doubly sure, we will label the लघु sound as ल, and the गुरु one as गा (not ग). Allow one and a half times as long to say the गा, as compared to ल.

☞ Remember that ल is *not* Long, but गा is Grand.

236

[You may entirely skip or forget this and the next paragraphs after reading them, unless you are planning to write poems in Sanskrit. Three syllables taken together constitute a group or गण, and it does not take a mathematical genius to figure out that there are eight (that is, 2³, or 2 x 2 x 2) possible sequences of ल and गा in various orders in a triplet, e.g., ललल, गागागा, लगाल, and so on, and so forth.

They are known (whimsically?) as य, म, त, र, ज, भ, न, स गणाः. We can append ल and गा to the list of गणाः to come up with the following mnemonic: यमाताराजभानसलगा, in which you can read यमाता, मातारा, ताराज, जभान, etc. ending in सलगा, to know the sequence of syllables. यमाता (ल-गा-गा) is य-गण, ताराज (गा-गा-ल) is त-गण, and so on.]

For the rest of us mortals, it is more practical to spell out the sequence using only ल and गा. I have used a slant (/) to indicate a pause to breathe. The pause may be filled by prolonging and petering off the pre-ceding vowel. You may want to try to say the meter using only ल and गा in proportioned duration, taking a brief pause (equivalent to ल), as indicated by a slant (/), if any. Then try to say or sing the श्लोक given as an example.

It is customary to identify the meter, in parentheses at the top of a stanza, or less commmonly, at the end of the stanza. You will automatically remember the names of various meters, provided you encounter them often. There is no explanation for how meters got their names. They have existed for hundreds of years.

First try to say the composition लगाललगा..... etc. out loud, three syllables or one गण at a time, allowing 50% longer duration for गा. After doing that a few times, you will figure out how to sing that meter, and will automatically remember it as well. Once you get the hang of it, you may try to read and/or sing the actual श्लोक. That's all there is to it.

The very first meter we'll talk about is the simplest, and the one that is most commonly used, अनुष्टुप्. Only for this meter, first read the श्लोक itself, rather than its composition — which looks complicated, but it is indeed very simple. Try the two-line format. It is, believe me, easier. There are four lines or पदाः in a stanza of any meter.

(अनुष्टुप्)
मा निषाद प्रतिष्ठां त्वम्
अगमः शाश्वतीः समाः ।
यत्क्रौंचमिथुनादेकम्
अवधीः काममोहितम् ॥   (रामायण)

The same may appear like this:

(अनुष्टुप्)
मा निषाद प्रतिष्ठां त्वमगमः शाश्वतीः समाः ।
यत्क्रौंचमिथुनादेकमवधीः काममोहितम् ॥   (रामायण)

> *"May you never get peace, o
> hunter, in that you killed one of the
> two Kraunch birds engrossed in love".*

Presumably, these are the spontaneous utterances of sage Valmiki, the author of the epic Ramayana. The unbearable anguish and anger felt on seeing one of a Kraunch birds who pair up for life, being killed by a hunter's arrow, took the form of the Anustup meter. This is believed to be the first poetic expression ever.

This is the commonest meter. It offers a great deal of flexibility, making it suitable to dialogues. In that, it reminds one of the Iambic (आयाम्बिक, not लाम्बिक) Pentameter of the English language. There are four lines, called पद (a foot, a step), each containing eight syllables, in any combination. An "X" below, indicates either ल or गा. However, the 5th letter is always a ल, the 6th one is always a गा, and the 7th one in 2nd and 4th lines is a ल, while in the 3rd line, it is a गा. For example, just see:

X X X X ल गा X X
X X X X ल गा ल X ।
X X X X ल गा गा X
X X X X ल गा ल X ॥

* *

(इन्द्रवज्रा)

गा॒ गा ल गा गा ल ल गा ल गा गा (११ अक्षराः)

अर्थो हि कन्या परकीय एव
तामद्य संप्रेष्य परिगृहीतुः ।
जातो ममायं विशदः प्रकामं
प्रत्यर्पितन्यासेवान्तरात्मा ॥

(अभिज्ञानशाकुंतल)

"A daughter is indeed, another's property. Having sent her today to her husband, my conscience is extremely calm, as it is when a deposit is returned to its owner".

These are the famous words of the sage Kanva, the foster father of Shakuntala, after bidding farewell to her.

Note that in this meter, the first अक्षर is always a गा, as opposed to the next otherwise identical meter, wherein the first अक्षर is a ल. A combination of these two meters follows the next one.

* *

(उपेन्द्रवज्रा)

ल॒ गा ल गा गा ल ल गा ल गा गा (११ अक्षराः)

रत्नैर्महार्हैस्तुतुषुर्न देवाः
न भेजिरे भीमविषेण भीतिम् ।
सुधां विना न प्रययुर्विरामम्
न निश्चितार्थाद्विरमन्ति धीराः ॥

(भर्तृहरि नीतिशतक)

"Gods were not satisfied with most precious jewels, nor were they afraid of terrible poison. They did not rest till they got the nectar of immortality. The steadfast ones do not rest before accomplishing their set objective".

239

This alludes to the mythological churning of the oceans by the gods to obtain the nectar of immortality, to win their eternal battle with the celestial bad guys. This story is detailed in the श्रीमद्भागवतम् which describes the incarnations of the Lord, — two such incarnations appear simultaneously in this event.

* *

(उपजाति)

गा॒ गा ल गा गा गा ल ल गा ल गा गा   (११ अक्षराः)
ल॒ गा ल गा गा गा ल ल गा ल गा गा   (११ अक्षराः)

स्वप्नो नु माया नु मतिभ्रमो नु
क्लिष्टं नु तावत्फलमेव पुण्यम् ।
असंनिवृत्त्यै तदतीतमेते
मनोरथा नाम तटप्रपाताः ॥   (अभिज्ञानशाकुंतल)

"Was it a dream or an illusion, or infatuation of mind,
        or the merit exhausted after giving just that amount of fruit?
        It is gone, never to return ever again. Indeed,
        these hopes are like the landslides off the river banks."

* *

(रथोद्धता)

गा ल गा ल ल ल गा ल गा ल गा   (११ अक्षराः)

आविवाहसमयाद् गृहे वने
शैशवे तदनु यौवने पुनः ।
स्वापहेतुरनुपाश्रितोऽन्यया
रामबाहुरुपधानमेष ते ॥   (उत्तररामचरित)

240

"Ever since the marriage, at home as well as in forest, during childhood and in youth, this arm of Rama, helping you to sleep, and on which no other woman has ever leaned, is indeed your pillow".

After defeating the demon रावण to reclaim सीता, Lord राम returned to their city अयोध्या. Now, राम offers his arm as a pillow to his beloved सीता, who is exhausted . राम is known for his devotion to only one woman, quite uncommon for a king in those days.

* *

(शालिनी)
गा गा गा गा / गा ल गा गा ल गा गा   (११ अक्षराः)

एको देवः केशवो वा शिवो वा
एकं मित्रं भूपतिर्वा यतिर्वा ।
एको वासः पत्तने वा वने वा
एका भार्या सुंदरी वा दरी वा ॥   (भर्तृहरि नीतिशतक)

"There ought to be only one God, either Keshav (Krishna) or Shiva; only one friend, a king or an ascetic; only one residence, a palace or a forest; only one wife, a beautiful damsel or a cave".

First of all, note the play of letters that are underlined. This श्लोकः sets forth mutually exclusive options in front of us. Wealth and salvation cannot go together. As the Bible says, *"It is easier for a camel to go through the eye of a needle, than for a wealthy man through the gates of heaven".*

Lord Krishna was a king, had many queens, and He preached the science of action कर्मयोग in भगवद्गीता. On the other hand, Lord Shiva is an ascetic, clad in only a loin cloth, his body smeared with ashes (burned and destroyed desires), and he lives in graveyards. भर्तृहरि respects either of them as leading one to salvation, but not both at the same time.

241

(स्वागता)
गा ल गा ल ल ल गा ल ल ल गा   (११ अक्षराः)

कुम्भपूरणभवः पटुरुद्वैर्
उच्चचार निनदोऽम्भसि तस्याः ।
तत्र स द्विरदबृंहितशंकी
शब्दपातिनमिषुं विससर्ज ॥   (रघुवंश)

"The sound of filling of the pot
reverberated into a loud roar over its
(the river Tamasa's) waters. Guessing
that it is a roar of an elephant, he (the
king Dasharatha) discharged an arrow
in the direction of the sound".

कालिदासस्य महाकाव्य रघुवंश deals with the entire dynasty of राम. रामायण
deals with His early and middle life, and   उत्तररामचरितम् by भवभूति deals
with the later part of His life.

This श्लोक describes how Rama's father King दशरथ, while he was
hunting, inadvertently killed श्रवणकुमार, the son of a blind ascetic elderly
couple on their pilgrimage. The boy's parents then put a curse on the king
to suffer the same fate, to die without any one of his four sons at his
side.

While भरत and शत्रुघ्न were away, राम and लक्ष्मण went to the forest
for twelve years, and दशरथ died when none of his four sons was around.
सीता was kidnapped by रावण, and was recovered after a battle, fought with
the help of the monkeys led by the great हनुमान. These characters are
allegorical.

राम had to abandon his dearest, and pregnant wife सीता to calm down
public opinion. सीता gave birth to his two sons in a hermitage. राम visits
that forest unaware of Sita's presence there, and is overcome by
memories or her. This is depicted in the play उत्तररामचरितम्. We will see a
few श्लोकाः from this play as well.

(तोटक)

ल ल गा ल ल गा ल ल गा ल ल गा   (१२ अक्षराः)

Note ललगा (स-गण) repeated four times.

स तथेति विनेतुरुदारमतेः
प्रतिगृह्य वचो विससर्ज मुनिम् ।
तदलब्धपदं हृदि शोकघने
प्रतिभातमिवान्तिकमस्य गुरोः ॥   (रघुवंश)

"Okay", said the king (Aja), accepting the consoling words of the generous sage (Vasishtha), and gave leave to his pupil. But these words, not finding room in the king's heart full of grief, as though went back to his preceptor".

Rama's ancestor Aja's wife had died, and a sage had sent his disciple with some wise words to console the king. He listened intently and thankfully, and bade farewell to the disciple. The grief overcame him promptly anyway. We will meet his wife इन्दुमती in the next section, to learn how they got married.

* *

(द्रुतविलम्बित)

ल ल ल गा ल ल गा ल ल गा ल गा   (१२ अक्षराः)

अयि कठोर यशः किल ते प्रियं
किमयशो ननु घोरमतः परम् ।
किमभवद्द्विपिने हरिणीदृशः
कथय नाथ कथं बत मन्यसे ॥   (उत्तररामचरितम्)

243

"Ah, ye ruthless, did you indeed seek fame? How much worse can infamy be than this? What happened to that fawn-eyed one (Sita) in the forest, pray tell me, O lord, what do you think?"

A friend chides Rama, who was compelled by his royal duties to give up his wife. This only deepens the pathos, since He never wanted to give her up anyway.

* *

(वंशस्थ)

ल गा ल गा गा ल ल गा ल गा ल गा   (१२ अक्षराः)

विचिन्तयन्ती यमनन्यमानसा
तपोधनं वेत्सि न मामुपस्थितम् ।
स्मरिष्यति त्वां न स बोधितोऽपि सन्
कथां प्रमत्तः प्रथमं कृतामिव ॥   (अभिज्ञानशाकुंतल)

"The person you are contemplating, with such concentration that you do not even recognize me— whose wealth is penance—, will not recognize you, even when reminded, just as an intoxicated person does not remember any previous talk".

Shakuntala's foster father sage Kanva was out of town, when king Dushyant came, fell in love with her, then left. She was in charge of the hermitage and of carrying out duties related to it. She was sitting alone, thinking about her departed lover, when sage Durvasa (known for his anger) paid a visit. On being ignored, he put a curse on her. Being in love is no excuse for neglecting one's duties.

* *

(प्रहर्षिणी)
गा गा गा ल ल ल ल गा ल गा ल गा गा   (१३ अक्षराः)

सख्युस्ते स किल शतक्रतोरजय्य
स्तस्य त्वं रणशिरसि स्मृतो निहन्ता ।
उच्छेतुं प्रभवति यन्न सप्तसप्ति-
स्तन्नैशं तिमिरमपाकरोति चन्द्रः ॥   (अभिज्ञानशाकुंतल)

> "They (the demons) are indeed
> unconquerable by your friend Indra; but
> you are considered to be their killer at
> the head of the battlefield. The Moon
> dispels darkness of the night, which
> the Sun is unable to drive away".

This request is addressed to the cursed Shakuntala's husband, King Dushyant, by a messenger of the king of the gods, Indra. The messenger diplomatically praises the king without belittling his own master. This is actually a ploy to take the king to where Shakuntala is.

* *

(मंजुभाषिणी)
ल ल गा ल गा ल / ल ल गा ल गा ल गा   (१३ अक्षराः)

परिपाण्डुदुर्बलकपोलसुन्दरं
दधती विलोलकबरीकमाननम् ।
करुणस्यमूर्तिरथवा शरीरिणी
विरहव्यथेव वनमेति जानकी ॥   (उत्तररामचरित)

> "Janaki (Sita, having emerged
> from the river Godawari, after bathing)
> is coming towards the forest. Her face,
> with a single dangling lock of hair,
> despite her emaciated, pale cheeks, is
> beautiful. She is the idol of pathos, or
> as if the pain of separation incarnate".

* *

(मत्तमयूर)

गा गा गा गा / गा ल ल गा गा ल ल गा गा   (१३ अक्षराः)

हा तातेति क्रन्दितमाकर्ण्य विषण्ण —
स्तस्यान्विष्यन्वेतसगूढं प्रभवं सः ।
शल्यप्रोतं प्रेक्ष्य सकुम्भं मुनिपुतं
तापादन्तः शल्य इवासीत्क्षितिपोऽपि ॥   (रघुवंश)

"Having heard a wail, 'O God !' he
(the King Dasharatha) was stunned. He
began looking for its origin in the deep
growth of reeds. On seeing the son of
the ascetic, pierced by the arrow, and
with a pitcher in his hand, the king was
full of misery, as if he himself was
pierced by the arrow".

* *

(वसन्ततिलका)

गा गा ल गा ल ल ल गा ल ल गा ल गा गा   (१४ अक्षराः)

रम्याणि वीक्ष्य मधुरांश्च निशम्य शब्दान्
पर्युत्सुकी भवति यत्सुखितोऽपि जन्तुः ।
तच्चेतसा स्मरति नूनमबोधपूर्वं
भावस्थिराणि जननान्तरसौहृदानि ॥   (अभिज्ञानशाकुंतल)

"On seeing beautiful objects, or
listening to sweet sounds, even a happy
person becomes restless. Then indeed
he remembers things not known before,
the associations of the past births
which are permanently impressed on
the soul".

* *

(मालिनी)

ल ल ल ल ल गा गा / गा ल गा गा ल गा गा (१५ अक्षराः)

सरसिजमनुविद्धं शैवलेनापि रम्यं
मलिनमपि हिमांशोर्लक्ष्म लक्ष्मीं तनोति ।
इयमधिकमनोज्ञा वल्कलेनापि तन्वी
किमिव हि मधुराणां मण्डनं नाकृतीनाम् ॥

(अभिज्ञानशाकुंतल)

"A lotus, even though covered by moss, is charming; the Moon, even though she is blemished, the blemish enhances her beauty; this young lady, even though clad in only a (tree) bark garment, is all the more enticing. What indeed is not an ornamentation to beautiful beings?"

* *

(पृथ्वी)

ल गा ल ल ल ल गा ल गा / ल ल ल गा ल गा गा ल गा (१७ अक्षराः)

श्रमाम्बुशिशिरीभवत्प्रसृतमन्दमन्दाकिनी
मरुत्तरलितालकालल्लाटचन्द्रद्युति ।
अकुंकुमकलंकितोज्ज्वलकपोलमुत्प्रेक्ष्यते
निराभरणसुन्दरश्रवणपाशमुग्धं मुखम् ॥

(उत्तररामचरित)

"Her face, —cool with drops of perspiration due to fatigue, with lustrous forehead covered by the curls of her hair, rendered tremulous by gentle breezes off the river Ganges, and with her resplendent cheeks, not smeared by saffron, and with her unadorned yet attractive ears, — as though it is in front of my eyes".

* *

247

(मन्दाक्रान्ता)

गा गा गा गा / ल ल ल ल ल गा / गा ल गा गा ल गा गा   (१७ अक्षराः)

वक्रः पन्था यदपि भवतः प्रस्थितस्योत्तराशां
सौधोत्संगप्रणयविमुखो मा स्म भूरुज्जयिन्याः ।
विद्युद्दामस्फुरितचकितैस्तत्र पौरांगनानां
लोलापांगैर्यदि न रमसे लोचनैर्वंचितोऽसि ॥   (मेघदूत)

"Even though that route may be circuitous for you, set out for the north,

do not be averse to aquainting youself with balconies of the city of Ujjain.

If you do not play with the tremulous angles (fleeting glances) of town women's eyes, dazed by the flashes of streaks of lightning,

(then) you might as well be devoid of eyes!"

A celestial male attendant of the treasurer of gods is cursed, by his master for ignoring assignments and spending time with his beloved wife instead, to spend one year in exile on the Earth, far away from his wife.

The year is almost over, and the monsoon begins. He sends a message to his beloved, with a rain cloud (मेघ) as a messenger (दूत), giving it detailed directions to follow, adding hints about sight-seeing along the way. कालिदास had done most of his famous work in the city of उज्जैन and undersatndably, was quite fond of it.

The entire poem मेघदूतम् by कालिदास is written in this meter. It is a slow, long, and deliberate meter. This meter is quite appropriate for depicting the agony of the star-crossed lover, and also the deliberate pace of his messenger embarking on a long and arduous journey.

* *

(शिखरिणी)

ल गा गा गा गा गा / ल ल ल ल ल गा / गा ल ल ल गा   (१७ अक्षराः)

अनाघ्रातं पुष्पं किसलयमलूनं कररुहै —
रनाविद्धं रत्नं मधु नवमनास्वादितरसम् ।
अखण्डं पुण्यानां फलमिव च तद्रूपमनघं
न जाने भोक्तारं कमिह समुपस्थास्यति विधिः ॥   (अभिज्ञानशाकुंतल)

     "Her faultless beauty is an unsmelt flower; a sprout unplucked by nail;

     a gem unperforated; fresh honey, its essence untasted;

     and is like the fruit of merits yet unexhausted.

     I don't know to whom the destiny will approach and ask to enjoy this".

* *

(हरिणी)

ल ल ल ल ल गा / गा गा गा गा / ल गा ल ल गा ल गा   (१७ अक्षराः)

न किल भवतां देव्याः स्थानं गृहेऽभिमतं तत-
स्तृणमिव वने शून्ये त्यक्ता न चाप्यनुशोचिता ।
चिरपरिचितास्ते ते भावाः परिद्रवयन्ति माम्
इयमशरणैरद्याप्येवं प्रसीदत रुद्यते ॥   (उत्तररामचरित)

     "(O people!), as you did not approve of her ladyship (my queen) staying at our home,

     I abandoned her in a desolate forest, like a worthless blade of grass, and didn't even grieve after her.

     However, now these erst-while familiar objects are melting me.

     Hence at last, here I am, helplessly crying. Please forgive me".

(शार्दूलविक्रीडित)

गा गा गा ल ल गा ल गा ल ल ल गा / गा गा ल गा गा ल गा (१९ अक्षराः)

पातुं न प्रथमं व्यवस्यति जलं युष्मास्वपीतेषु या
नादत्ते प्रियमण्डनापि भवतां स्नेहेन या पल्लवम् ।
आद्ये वः कुसुमप्रसूतिसमये यस्या भवत्युत्सवः
सेयं याति शकुन्तला पतिगृहं सर्वैरनुज्ञायताम् ॥   (अभिज्ञानशाकुंतल)

> "She never drinks water, before
> you are watered;
> although fond of ornaments, she
> never plucks a leaf, due to affection
> for you;
> the time of your first blossom is
> a festive occasion for her.
> That Shakuntala is going to her
> husband's house. May you all give her
> your leave".

* *

(स्रग्धरा)

गा गा गा गा ल गा गा / ल ल ल ल ल ल गा / गा ल गा गा ल गा गा (२१ अक्षराः)

जीर्णा कन्था ततः किं सितममलपटं पट्टसूत्रं ततः किम्
एका भार्या ततः किं हयकरिसुगणैरावृतो वा ततः किम् ।
भक्तं भुक्तं ततः किं कदशनमथवा वासरान्ते ततः किम्
व्यक्तज्योतिर्न चान्तर्मथितभवभयं वैभवं वा ततः किम् ॥   (भर्तृहरि वैराग्यशतक)

> "If there is a torn, patched
> garment, or if there is a clean, white,
> silk garment, so what?
>
> If there is only a wife, or if (one
> is) surrounded by multitude of horses
> and elephants, so what?

If there is a dinner of rice, or if there is some poor food at the end of the day, so what?

If there is no realization of the inner light, breaking the cycle of re-births, then if there are all material pleasures of the world, so what?"

* *

This concludes our discussion of the Meters. I hope you enjoyed it. It would be nice if you can now identify the meters of the श्लोका: we have seen earlier, and can attempt to sing them. Nothing is lost, if you can not do that. The real treasures are the श्लोका: themselves, and not their meters. New श्लोका: were selected, just for enhancing your appreciation of the classical संस्कृत literature.

Admittedly, these श्लोका: were difficult to read, but that shouldn't have dampened your fun. Once you know the meaning, you can go back to the original, and appreciate it still more. Some of the meters are unfamiliar to myself as well. Therefore, I have had the same pleasure of adventure that you had.

The same will hold true for what is to come in the next section. You have nearly reached the top of the mountain. The climb was arduous, and you may feel a bit exhausted. No, you are not out of breath. You are breathing a new life, and are only aware of it.

Admire the view around you. Rest for a while, and look back to see how high you have already come. Compliment yourself on successfully climbing over one after another, apparently intimidating hilltops you have left behind.

And most important of all, continue to look upwards. This is not the end. The journey has only begun. When you reach the top, you will see "mountains over mountains arise", each one being more enticing than the one just before it.

FIGURES OF SPEECH अलंकाराः

You are quite familiar with *Parts of Speech,* viz., Nouns, Adjectives, Conjunctions, and so on. Various ornaments that the language may put on to look more attractive are called *Figures of Speech.* These include, Simile, Metaphor, Alliteration, Generalization, onomatoeia, etc. Sanskrit has an over abundance of all of these अलंकाराः to delight you. Don't let them scare you. Remember, she is trying to attract you !

Continue to focus on fun and appreciation. Concentrate on the Sanskrit text, and try to see the points of interest being pointed out to you. Names of various figures of speech are for identification only. You do not have to compare and contrast their characteristics. Their description will highlight their features.

As was the case with the section on the Meters, only the relevant meaning and context are provided. Several of these figures of speech work better on a particular cultural background, making their translation especially demanding to do, and difficult to understand. So, only the fun part follows.

अलंकाराः may depend upon actually looking at, or listening to the written or the spoken word (शब्दालंकार), or upon the meaning of words (अर्थालंकार).

* *

शब्दालंकाराः

अनुप्रास (Alliteration) — Repetition of one or more syllables.

एते ते कुहरेषु गद्गदनदद्गोदावरीवारयो   (उत्तररामचरित)

The repetition of ग, द, व, and र, re-creates the sound of rushing waters of the river गोदावरी. Another example, the ल sound appears eleven times in the following line.

(स्रग्धरा)
आमूलालोलधूली बहुलपरिमला लीढलोलालीमाला   (संसारदावानल स्तोत्र)

यमक — Repetition of words or syllables similar in sound, but different in meaning, a rhyme of different sorts.

विजयदुन्दुभितां ययुरुर्णवा घनर<u>वा</u> नर<u>वा</u>हनसंपदः

The pair of syllables र वा is repeated, but it means altogether different things each time; घनरवा is sound of thunder, while नरवाहन is the treasurer of gods. In the previous section, we saw सुंदरी <u>वा</u> दरी <u>वा</u>.

* *

अर्थालंकाराः

उपमा — When you compare your daily life to a rat-race, it is called a Simile, that is, a comparison. In Sanskrit, it is called उपमा. The great कालिदास was a master of उपमा.

(उपजाति)
संचारिणी दीपशिखेव रात्रौ
यं यं व्यतीयाय पतिंवरा सा
नरेन्द्रमार्गाट्ट इव प्रपेदे
विवर्णभावं स स भूमिपालः ॥   (रघुवंश)

"Moving along, like light from a lamp at night,
Whom whom passes by the suitor she;
Like the store-fronts along a market street,
Lusterless became such such king's faces !"

Princess Indumati's parents have invited eligible royal princes and kings to claim her hand in matrimony. All suitors are seated in a row. The princess knows a lot about them, but has not seen them before.

She is to walk in front of them, with a garland ("wedding ring") in her hands, looking at each one of them carefully, raising their expectations. As she comes closer to them, their faces brighten up. But, just as she passes them by, their faces lose all their radiance and glory.

The poet compares this situation with someone walking down the market street, with a lantern in hand. Turrets approached by the lantern light up, and as the lantern moves away, they fall back into darkness.

Faces of assembled suitors are compared to shops and turrets. That is nothing great. However, the princess is like the flame of the lamp. Imagine a slim and tall, delicate and translucent candle walking by. दीपशिखा means "tip of the wick" (flame) of a lamp.

The princess Indumati chose अज, Rama's ancestor, whom we saw in the previous section grieving over the same Indumati's death.

* *

अनन्वय — When a thing is compared with itself.

गगनं गगनाकारं सागरः सागरोपमः ।
रामरावणयोर्युद्धं रामरावणयोरिव ॥   (कुवलयानन्द)

The sky is said to be like the sky, the ocean like the ocean, and the battle between राम and रावण like itself. उपमेय or the object of comparison, and उपमान or the standard of comparison are identical. Do not confuse अनन्वय with अन्वय (modern word order), or with अव्यय (non-changing words).

* *

ससंदेह — Similarity between उपमेय and उपमान makes one
        wonder, as to whether the object is itself or
        something else.

आक्ष्योतनं नु हरिचंदनपल्लवानां
निष्पीडितेन्दुकरकन्दलजो नु सेकः ।
आतप्तजीवितपुनःपरितर्पणोऽयं
संजीवनौषधिरसो नु हृदि प्रसक्तः ॥   (उत्तररामचरित)

राम regains consciousness after सीता caresses him. राम does not know that सीता was present there. The thrill of his delight is expressed in a series of doubts: Is the touch that of the soothing sap of Harichandan leaves? Is it a spray of cool rays of Moon? Is it the extract of some life-giving herb?

* *

उत्प्रेक्षा — When the present object उपमेय is fancied as the other उपमान. "As if" is the hallmark of this अलंकारः

लिम्पतीव तमोंऽगानि वर्षतीवांजनं नभः ।   (मृच्छकटिक)

This is a description of a dark night. As if the sky is showering a rain of black collyrium, painting the body black!

* *

भ्रान्तिमान् — When the similarity between the उपमेय and the उपमान leads to mistaking one for the other.

We saw the श्लोकः, "कुम्भपूरण...." in the previous section, regarding how King दशरथ mistook श्रवणकुमार, filling his jug with water, for a grunting elephant, and killed him.

Not all kinds of confusion and mistaken identities would qualify for this designation. Another example of this अलंकार appears in the Preface. A famous writer Mr. Kalelkar says:

"Thinking of glowing gems of Sanskrit
to be burning charcoals, people stay away
from that language".

* *

रूपक — When you use the term "rat-race" *instead of* your daily life, as in, "When shall this rat-race end?", you are using a Metaphor. The Sanskrit word for that is रूपक (रूप = a form, a shape). The following सुभाषितम् is studded with दृष्टांताः (examples) of रूपक अलंकार ।

आशा नाम नदी मनोरथजला तृष्णातरंगाकुला
राग‌ग्राहवती वितर्कविहगा धैर्यद्रुमध्वंसिनी ।
मोहावर्तसुदुस्तरातिगहना प्रोत्तुंगचिन्तातटी
तस्याः पारगता विशुद्धमनसो नन्दन्ति योगीश्वराः ॥   (भर्तृहरि वैराग्यशतक)

"This river called Hope, with
water of fantasy, waves of desires,
        With crocodiles of attachment,
flying birds of doubts, uprooting the
tree of patience.
        With a very deep, impossible-to-
swim whirl of infatuation and
confusion, and with steep banks of
worries.
        Having crossed this river, pure-
minded master Yogis take delight".

Another excellent example:

त्वं जीवितं त्वमसि मे हृदयं द्वितीयं
त्वं कौमुदी नयनयोरमृतं त्वमंगे ।   (उत्तररामचरित)

राम identifies सीता with जीवित (his life), हृदय (heart), कौमुदी
(Moonlight), and अमृत (nectar of immortality).

* *

अतिशयोक्ति — When the imagined description is based on
hyperbole, or exaggeration. The intention here is to
praise, not to deceive. Therefore, not all
outrageous claims would qualify as this अलंकार.

उदेति पूर्वं कुसुमं ततः फलं
घनोदयं प्राक्तदनंतरं पयः ।
निमित्तनैमित्तिकयोरयं क्रम -
स्तव प्रसादस्य पुरस्तु संपदः ॥   (अभिज्ञानशाकुन्तल)

The normal order of cause and effect is, first the appearance of flower and then the fruit, first the amassing of the clouds and then the rain-shower. But here the exaggeration is, that the effect, prosperity, precedes the favor of the sage Maricha, whose imminent favor is enough.

* *

अपह्नुति (अपह्नुति) — When two objects have some similarity between them and the object of description उपमेय is denied to be what it is, and is stated to be another thing उपमान instead.

नैता प्रियतमा वाचः
स्नेहार्द्रा शोक्दारुणाः ।
एतास्ता मधुनो धाराः
श्योतन्ति सविषास्त्वयि ॥ (उत्तररामचरित)

Sorrowful words of राम expressing his deep love for सीता are described as resembling streams of honey mixed with poison. Honey, because of confession of unchangable love; and poison, because of the fear that the heart-rending grief of राम might endanger his life. But this resemblance is expressed by denying the उपमेय (वाचः speech) and asserting the उपमान (मधुनो धाराः streams of honey).

* *

तुल्ययोगिता — When several things are connected with a single common property.

न प्रमाणीकृतः पाणिः बाल्ये बालेन पीडितः ।
नाहं न जनको नाग्निर्नानुवृत्तिर्न संततिः ॥ (उत्तररामचरित)

सीता was mythologically daughter of the Earth, and was brought up by king जनक. The above is said by the Earth regarding the abandoning of सीता by राम. Here several things and persons — पाणि (the hand) of सीता that राम took in their marriage, अहम् (the Earth herself), king जनक, literally her "father", अग्नि (the fire which proved Sita's chastity in the ordeal of her trial by fire), अनुवृत्ति (Sita's obedient nature), and संतति (prospective progeny) are all connected by a single property: न प्रमाणीकृतः (the authority was disregarded), even though each one of them is प्रस्तुत or relevant, being a factor for establishing Sita's purity.

* *

दृष्टांत — When there is a reflective corresponence
between the उपमेय and the उपमान.

कामं नृपाः सन्तु सहस्रशोऽन्ये
राजन्वतीमाहुरनेन भूमिम् ।
नक्षत्रताराग्रहसंकुलाऽपि
ज्योतिष्मती चन्द्रमसैव रात्रिः ॥   (रघुवंश)

There is a perfect correspondence between these two sets of elements: The Earth is compared to the night; thousands of kings ruling over the Earth correspond to the constellations, stars, and planets with which the sky is studded; the king परंतप of मगध is being described as the Moon; and the property "possessed of a good king" (राजन्वती) attributed to the Earth corresponds to "possessed of bright light" (ज्योतिष्मती), which is attributed to the night.

* *

निदर्शना — When an apparently impossible connection
between things leads to the suggestion of
similarity.

इदं किलाव्याजमनोहरं वपु-
स्तपक्षमं साधयितुं य इच्छति ।
ध्रुवं स नीलोत्पलपत्रधारया
शमीलतां छेत्तुमृषिर्व्यवस्यति ॥   (अभिज्ञानशाकुंतल)

This is said by दुष्यन्त about sage कण्व, on seeing शकुन्तला watering the trees in the hermitage. There are two statements here: Making her body fit for practicing penance; and cutting the शमी creeper with the blade of a blue lotus leaf. There is no connection between these two ideas. However, when they are put together, there is a clear suggestion of similarity. "What a waste !" applies to either action.

* *

समासोक्ति — When description of what is relevant प्रस्तुत,
  suggests what is not relevant अप्रस्तुत.

उपोढरागेण विलोलतारकं
तथा गृहीतं शशिना निशामुखम् ।
यथा समस्तं तिमिरांशुकं तथा
पुरोऽपि रागाह्नलितं न लक्षितम् ॥

The Moon (Masculine gender in संस्कृत) is holding the face of the night, and the night does not even realize that her garment of darkness is slipping off her body entirely. The implication is, the garment of the beloved is slipping off her body engaged in dalliance with her lover.

* *

अप्रस्तुतप्रशंसा — When the description (प्रशंसा "Praise") of the
  irrelevant (अप्रस्तुत) matter is given, in order to
  suggest the प्रस्तुत.

अभिनवमधुलोलुपस्त्वं तथा परिचुम्ब्य चूतमंजरीम् ।
कमलवसतिमात्रनिर्वृतो मधुकर विस्मृतोऽस्येनां कथम् ॥   (अभिज्ञानशाकुंतल)

This is the famous song of the queen हंसपदिका. The description of a honey bee, going from one flower to another, which is not really relevant suggests दुष्यन्त who had left हंसपदिका and was living with वसुमती. There is a further suggestion, by extrapolation, that he had forgotten शकुंतला as well. The analogous pairs are: मधुकर—दुष्यन्त; चूतमंजरी (mango blossom)— हंसपदिका, शकुन्तला; and कमल—वसुमती.

* *

259

व्यतिरेक — When excellence or superiority of the object
उपमेय prevails over the उपमान.

वज्रादपि कठोराणि मृदूनि कुसुमादपि ।
लोकोत्तराणां चेतांसि को हि विज्ञातुमर्हति ॥ (उत्तररामचरित)

वज्र (adamant, or a thunderbolt) and कुसुम (flower) are the usual उपमान
for comparing hardness and softness respectively. But the उपमेय, that is,
hearts of extraordinary men are stated to be harder than वज्र, and yet,
softer than कुसुम.

* *

विरोध —When apparently there is a contradiction in the
statement, though no contradiction really exists.

या निशा सर्वभूतानां तस्यां जागर्ति संयमी ।
यस्यां जाग्रति भूतानि सा निशा पश्यतो मुनेः ॥ (भगवद्गीता)

Here the apparent contradiction lies in the fact that the "day" of
ordinary men is the "night" of the discerning (पश्यतः) sage, and their "night"
is his "day". This apparent contradiction is explained by taking the "day" to
signify light of knowledge, and the "night" signifying the darkness of
ignorance. Ordinary people keep themselves busy with things that a
discerning one avoids, and vice versa.

* *

विषम — When there is dissimilarity or incongruity,
either in the nature of things or in the sphere of
causal relation.

दलति हृदयं गाढोद्वेगं द्विधा न तु भिद्यते
वहति विकलः कायो मोहं न मुंचति चेतनाम् ।
ज्वलयति तनूमन्तर्दाहः करोति न भस्मसात्
प्रहरति विधिर्मर्मच्छेदी न कृन्तति जीवितम् ॥ (उत्तररामचरित)

260

राम is describing his agony stemming from separation from सीता. Now his heart is torn (दलति "splits"), but it does not separate into two parts (द्विधा न भिद्यते); the body swoons (मोहं वहति), but the consciousness does not disappear (चेतना न मुंचति); the fire of sorrow burns the body, but does not reduce it to ashes (भस्मसात् न करोति); the Fate strikes hard, but it does not cut off the life (जीवितं न कृन्तति) !

* *

विभावना — When the effect takes place in the absence of its cause.

प्रसाद इव मूर्तस्ते स्पर्शः स्नेहार्द्रशीतलः ।
अद्याप्यानन्दयति मां त्वं पुनः क्वासि नन्दिनी ॥   (उत्तररामचरित)

This is addressed to the invisible सीता by राम. The effect, namely the sensation of delight (अद्यापि मां आनन्दयति) is stated to be present, but its cause, the "pleaser" (नन्दिनी-सीता) is not to be seen (त्वं क्व असि ? Where are you ?).

* *

असंगति — When two qualities related as cause and effect
          are mentioned as residing in separate places.

अहो खलभुजंगस्य विचित्रोऽयं वधक्रमः ।
अन्यस्य दशति श्रोत्रमन्यः प्राणैर्विमुच्यते ॥   (भर्तृहरि)

The nature of a wicked man is described by contrasting the effect of his behavior with that of a serpent. The wicked man bites the ear of one person, but that makes someone else die! The cause (दशनं - "biting", pouring poison in the ear) belongs in one place, but its effect (प्राणवियोग - death) happens in a different place.

* *

261

स्वभावोक्ति — A realistic and vivid description, a character statement (उक्ति) of one's inherent nature (स्व-भाव).

ग्रीवाभंगाभिरामं मुहुरनुपतति स्यन्दने वक्रदृष्टिम्
पश्चार्धेन प्रविष्टः शरपतनभयाद् भूयसा पूर्वकायम् ।
दर्भैरर्धावलीढैः श्रमविवृतमुखभ्रंशिभिः कीर्णवर्त्मा
पश्योदग्रप्लुतत्वाद्वियति बहुतरं स्तोकमुर्व्यां प्रयाति ॥   (अभिज्ञान शाकुंतल)

This is the most picturesque description of the deer running to save his life from the hunter दुष्यन्त coming after him in a chariot. Graceful, owing to the bending of the neck, hinder part of his body contracted into the fore part for the fear of the arrow, scattering along the path, half-chewed grass dropping from his mouth because of exhaustion. The last line is a beautiful exanmple of उत्प्रेक्षा — *as if* with his high leaps, he moves more in the sky and less on the ground.

* *

अर्थान्तरन्यास   (*Generalization*) — When a particular statement is supported by the general, or a general one by the particular.

Many of the श्लोकाः we have seen so far, set their premise in the first three lines, by giving examples, and then state the conclusion or inference in the fourth line. You may remember one such सुभाषित,

उदये सविता रक्तो रक्तश्चास्तमने तथा ।
संपत्तौ च विपत्तौ च महतामेकरूपता ।

Here is a new example:

स्त्रीणामशिक्षितपटुत्वममानुषीषु
संदृश्यते किमुत या प्रतिबोधवत्यः ।
प्रागन्तरिक्षगमनात्स्वमपत्यजातम्
अन्यैर्द्विजैः परभृता खलु पोषयन्ति ॥   (अभिज्ञानशाकुन्तल)

This is a famous verse in which दुष्यन्त casts aspersion on the entire womankind. शकुन्तला, carrying a child of दुष्यन्त, leaves the sage कण्व and others and comes to the court of दुष्यन्त, who under the spell of the curse, fails to recognize शकुन्तला, who then mentions his unborn child to refresh his memory.

There is a general condemnation of women in the first half of the verse. Intuitive cunning is present even in non-human females, then what to speak of those endowed with reason (possibly far more so)? He supports his generalization with a particular example that the female cuckoo birds get their young ones reared by the crows and other unsuspecting birds.

* *

श्लेष —You are quite familiar with श्लेष or the "pun". It is more commonly used in prose or गद्य, rather than in poetry or पद्य.

There are many more अलंकाराः, but there is no need for you to remember or even to know their names. The same is true for the समासाः or words joined together. Some day, you may want to learn all that, and have more fun. Now you are ready to appreciate the beauty of all the श्लोकाः we have seen in this tribute to the संस्कृत language, without any apprehension. Have fun !

श्लोकाः *That You Already Know*

In case you hadn't noticed before reaching The Treasure Chest, we had studied in detail, many श्लोकाश्च सुभाषितानि च in parts II and III as well. Lest one may conclude that all those श्लोकाः were anything but the real gems, it is better to list them as treasures, too!

Those श्लोकाः and सुभाषितानि are reproduced below in the order in which they appeared in the text, with the page पृष्ठ on which they appeared, making them easy to locate. I would like you to read them, and see whether you can make any sense out of them. One caveat, though. Don't use your memory aggressively. Don't strain it to sqeeze out the meaning. That would be intuitive, but counter-productive (that is, you will feel like doing that, but don't) !

Like our test drive of a new car, this is also a test. But it is a test of my ability to teach without any tension on your part, rather than a test of your otherwise excellent memory. You can never fail. And I had lot of fun along the way. Why else would I do all this!

My suggestion is, muster all the skills you have acquired, and try to find out the nouns, verbs, their derivatives — declensions and conjugations — then the modern word order or अन्वय, and finally, the meaning. Having attempted that, if it is still necessary, you can return to the earlier pages and go over the श्लोक and the accompanying explanations again. That is not a failure. Perseverance is the only way to succeed. प्रयत्नं सततं कुर्वाणो संपदं लभते नरः !

You may find it hard to believe that you already possess a treasure cove of more than one hundred gems — 110 श्लोकाः and 30 श्लोकार्धाः to be exact ! शुभं भवतु !

Index of Shloka from the Text Parts I-III

श्लोक / सुभाषित   पृष्ठ

(वसंततिलका)
पापान्निवारयति योजयते हिताय
गुह्यां च गूहति गुणान्प्रकटीकरोति ।
आपन्नं च न जहाति ददाति काले
सन्मित्रलक्षणमिदं प्रवदन्ति सन्तः ॥   Dedication

(अनुष्टुप)
यथा चित्तं तथा वाचा यथा वाचा तथा क्रिया ।
चित्ते वाचि क्रियायां च महतां एकरूपता ॥   63

(अनुष्टुप)
गंगा पापं, शशि तापं दैन्यं कल्पतरुस्तथा ।
पापं, तापं च दैन्यं च घ्नन्ति संतो महाशयाः ॥   73

(उपजाति)
कायेन वाचा मनसेन्द्रियैर्वा
बुद्ध्यात्मना वा प्रकृतेः प्रभावात् ।
करोमि यद्यत्सकलं परस्मै
नारायणायेव समर्पयामि ॥   75

(उपेन्द्रवज्रा)
श्री कृष्ण ! गोविंद ! हरे ! मुरारे !
हे नाथ ! नारायण ! वासुदेव !   78

(अनुष्टुप)
आकाशात्पतितं तोयं यथा गच्छति सागरम् ।
सर्व देव नमस्कारः केशवं प्रति गच्छति ॥   95

(अनुष्टुप)
जगतः पितरौ वंदे पार्वतीपरमेश्वरौ !   99

(उपजाति)
विद्या विवादाय धनं मदाय
शक्तिः परेषां परपीडनाय ।
खलस्य साधोः विपरीतमेतत्
ज्ञानाय दानाय च रक्षणाय ॥   106

(अनुष्टुप)
उत्सवे व्यसने चैव दुर्भिक्षे शत्रुविग्रहे ।
राजद्वारे स्मशाने च यः तिष्ठति सः बांधवः ॥   109

(अनुष्टुप)
उद्यमेन हि सिध्यन्ति कार्याणि न मनोरथैः ।
न हि सुप्तस्य सिंहस्य प्रविशन्ति मुखे मृगाः ॥   113

(अनुष्टुप्)
सर्पदुर्जनयोर्मध्ये वरं सर्पो न दुर्जनः ।
सर्पो दसति कालेन दुर्जनस्तु पदे पदे ॥ 115

(अनुष्टुप्)
गुरुर्ब्रह्मा गुरुर्विष्णुर्गुरुर्देबो महेश्वरः । 117
गुरुः साक्षात्परबह्म तस्मै श्री गुरुवे नमः ॥

(अनुष्टुप्)
ध्यायतः विषयान्पुंसः संगस्तेषूपजायते ।
संगात्संजायते कामः कामात्क्रोधोऽभिजायते ॥ 118
क्रोधाद्भवति संमोह संमोहात्स्मृतिविभ्रमः ।
स्मृतिभ्रंशात्बुद्धिनाशो बुद्धिनाशात्प्रणश्यति ॥ 123

(शार्दूलविक्रीडित)
वीरः सर्व सुरासुरेन्द्रमहितो वीरं बुधाः संश्रिताः
वीरेणाभिहतः स्वकर्म निचयो वीराय नित्यं नमः ।
वीरात्तीर्थमिदं प्रवृत्तमतुलम् वीरस्य घोरं तपो
वीरे श्री धृति कीर्ति कांति निचयः श्री वीरः भद्रं दिश ॥ 126

(शार्दूलविक्रीडित)
रामो राजमणि सदा विजयते रामं रमेशं भजे
रामेणाभिहता निशाचरचमूः रामाय तस्मै नमः ।
रामान्नास्ति परायणं परतरं रामस्य दासोस्म्यहम्
रामे चित्तलयः सदा भवतु मे भो राम ! मामुद्धर ! 128

(अनुष्टुप्)
नैनं छिंदन्ति शस्त्राणि नैनं दहति पावकः ।
न चैनं क्लेदयन्त्यापो न शोषयति मारुतः ॥ 132

(वंसस्थ)
न जायते म्रियते वा कदाचित् (a quarter stanza) 133

(अनुष्टुप्)
नमो नमस्ते भगवन् ! दीनानां शरणं प्रभो । 135
नमस्ते करुणासिन्धो ! नमस्ते मोक्षदायक ॥

(मालिनी)
करचरणकृतं वाक्कायजं कर्मजं वा । 135
श्रवणनयनजं वा मानसं वाऽपराधम् ॥
विदितमविदितं वा सर्वमेतत्क्षमस्व । 137
जय जय करुणाब्धे ! श्री महादेव शंभो ॥

जय जय करुणाब्धे ! सच्चिदानंददेव ! 140

सा विद्या या विमुक्तये । 143

(अनुष्टुप्)
तद्विद्धिप्रणिपातेन परिप्रश्नेन सेवया 144

(अनुष्टुप्)
न हि ज्ञानेन सदृशं पवित्रं इह विद्यते । 144

(अनुष्टुप्)
यत्करोषि यदश्नासि यज्जुहोषि ददासि यत्।
यत्तपस्यसि कौन्तेय ! तत्कुरुष्व मद्‌र्पणम् ॥   154

(अनुष्टुप्)
यदा यदा हि धर्मस्य ग्लानिर्भवति भारत ।
अभ्युत्थानमधर्मस्य तदात्मानं सृजाम्यहम् ॥
परित्राणाय साधूनां विनाशाय च दुष्कृताम् ।
धर्मसंस्थापनार्थाय संभवामि युगे युगे ॥   156

(अनुष्टुप्)
विद्वत्वं च नृपत्वं च नैव तुल्यं कदाचन ।
स्वदेशे पूज्यते राजा विद्वान्सर्वत्र पूज्यते ॥   162

सत्यमेव जयते नानृतम्।   163

एकं सद्विप्राः बहुधा वदन्ति ।   164

(वसंततिलका)
प्रारभ्यते न खलु विघ्नभयेन नीचैः
प्रारभ्य विघ्नविहता विरमन्ति मध्याः ।
विघ्नैः पुनः पुनरपि प्रतिहन्यमाना
प्रारब्धमुत्तमजना न परित्यजन्ति ॥   169

यद्यपि सत्यं लोकविरुद्धं ना करणीयं नाचरणीयम्।   175

(तोटक)
शशिना च निशा निशया च शशि
शशिना निशया च विभाति नभः ।
पयसा कमलं कमलेन पयः
पयसा कमलेन विभाति सरः ॥   179

(उपजाति)
अस्त्युत्तरस्यां दिशि देवतात्मा
हिमालयो नाम नगाधिराजः ।   181

(अनुष्टुप्)
आपदामपहर्तारं दातारं सर्व संपदाम्।
लोकाभिरामं श्री रामं भूयो भूयो नमाम्यहम् ॥   183

(अनुष्टुप्)
उदये सविता रक्तो रक्तश्चास्तमने तथा ।
संपत्तौ च विपत्तौ च महतां एकरूपता ॥   184

(अनुष्टुप्)
प्रयत्नं सततं कुर्वाणो संपदं लभते नरः ।   186

(अनुष्टुप्)
जननी जन्मभूमिश्च स्वर्गादपि गरीयसी ।   187

(वंशस्थ)
न चैतद्विद्वः कतरन्नो गरीयो
यद्वा जयेम यदि वा नो जयेयुः ।
यानेव हत्वा न जिजिविषामः
तेऽवस्थिता प्रमुखे धार्तराष्ट्राः ॥ 188

यां चिन्तयामि सततं मयि सा विरक्ता
साप्यन्यमिच्छति जनं स जनोऽन्यसक्तः ।
अस्मत्कृते च परितुष्यति काचिदन्या
धिक् तां च तं च मदनं च इमां च मां च ॥ 191

यूयं वयं वयं यूयमित्यासिन्मतिरावयोः ।
किं जातमधुना येन यूयं यूयं वयं वयम् ॥ 194

त्वमेव माता च पिता त्वमेव
त्वमेव बंधुश्च सखा त्वमेव ।
त्वमेव विद्या द्रविणं त्वमेव
त्वमेव सर्वं मम देवदेव ॥ 197

तुभ्यं नमस्त्रिभुवनार्तिहराय नाथ !
तुभ्यं नमः क्षितितलामलभूषणाय ।
तुभ्यं नमस्त्रिजगतः परमेश्वराय
तुभ्यं नमो जिन ! भवोदधिशोषणाय ! ॥ 197

(अनुष्टुप्)
भाषासु मुख्या मधुरा दिव्या गीर्वाणभारती ।
तस्माद्धि काव्यं मधुरं तस्मादपि सुभाषितम् ॥ 201

(अनुष्टुप्)
यस्य नास्ति स्वयं प्रज्ञा शास्त्रं तस्य करोति किम् ?
लोचनाभ्यां विहीनस्य दर्पणः किं करिष्यति ? 202

(इन्द्रवज्रा)
रात्रिर्गमिष्यति भविष्यति सुप्रभातम् ।
भास्वानुदेष्यति हसिष्यति पंकजश्री ॥ 205

(अनुष्टुप्)
मामकाः पांडवाश्चैव किमकुर्वत संजय । 207

(अनुष्टुप्)
सत्यं ब्रूयात्प्रियं ब्रूयान्नब्रूयात्सत्यमप्रियम् ।
प्रियं च नानृतं ब्रूयादेषः धर्मः सनातनः ॥ 209

अति सर्वत्र वर्जयेत् । 210
सत्यं वद ! धर्मं चर ! 210
प्रसीद ! 210
शुभं भवतु ! 210

कराग्रे वसते लक्ष्मी करमूले सरस्वती ।
करमध्ये तु गोविंदः प्रभाते करदर्शनम् ॥ 211

First-Line Index of The Treasure Chest

षड् दोषाः पुरुषेणेह 218
श्लोकस्थान सहस्त्राणि 218
मातृवत् परदारेषु 218
येषां न विद्या न तपो न दानं 219
विद्या नाम नरस्य रूपमधिकं प्रच्छन्नगुप्तं धनम् 219
ऐश्वर्यस्य विभूषणं सुजनता शौर्यस्य वाक्संयमो 220
न सा सभा यत्र न सन्ति वृद्धा 220
सुलभाः पुरुषाः लोके 221
जाड्यं धियो हरति सिंचति वाचि सत्यं 221
नास्ति कामसमो व्याधिः 221
अज्ञानतिमिरांधानां 222
गुरुर्ब्रह्मा गुरुर्विष्णु- 222

पिबन्ति नद्यः स्वयमेव नाम्भः 223
धैर्य यस्य पिता क्षमा च जननी शांतिश्चिरं गेहिनी 223
श्रुतिर्विभिन्ना स्मृतयश्च भिन्ना 223
वज्रादपि कठोराणि मृदूनि कुसुमादपि । 224
निन्दन्तु नीतिनिपुणाः यदि वा स्तुवन्तु 225
वांछा सज्जनसंगमे परगुणे प्रीतिर्गुरौ नम्रता 225
घृष्टं घृष्टं पुनरपि पुनश्चंदनं चारुगंधं 225

मूलं भुजंगैः शिखरं प्लवंगैः 226
सा विद्या या विमुक्तये ! 226
शिवास्ते पंथानः सन्तु ! 226
शतं जीव शरदः ! 226
मातृ देवो भव ! 226
क्षणे क्षणे यन्नवतामुपैति 227
मुक्ताफलेषु छायायाः 227
वंदे मातरम् । वंदे मातरम् । 228

ॐ सहनाववतु । 229
असतो मा सद् गमय ! 229
यं ब्रह्मा वरुणेन्द्र रुद्र मरुतः स्तुन्वन्ति दिव्यैस्तवैः 230
वक्रतुंड ! महाकाय ! 230
या कुंदेन्दु तुषारहार धवला या शुभ्रवस्त्रावृता 230
तुभ्यं नमस्त्रिभुवनार्तिहराय नाथ ! 231
शांताकारं भुजगशयनं पद्मनाभं सुरेश्वम् 232
मूकं करोति वाचाल 232
करारविंदेन पदारविंदं 233
समुद्रवसने देवि ! 233

छंदाः   मा निषाद प्रतिष्ठां त्वम् 238
अर्थो हि कन्या परकीय एव 239
रत्नैर्महार्हैस्तुतुषुर्न देवाः 239
स्वप्नो नु माया नु मतिभ्रमो नु 240
आविवाहसमयाद् गृहे वने 240

एको देवः केशवो वा शिवो वा   241

कुम्भपूरणभवः पटुरुत्रैर्   242

स तथेति विनेतुरुष्टारमतेः   243

अयि कठोर यज्ञः किल ते प्रियं   243

विचिन्तयन्ती यमनन्यमानसा   244

सख्युस्ते स किल ऋतक्रतोरजव्य   245

परिपाण्डुदुर्बलकपोलसुन्दरं   245

हा तातेति क्रन्दितमाकर्ण्य विषण्ण   246

रम्याणि वीक्ष्य मधुराश्च निशम्य शल्यान्   246

सरसिजमनुविद्धं शैवलेनापि रम्यं   247

श्रमाम्बुशिश्रीरीभवत्प्रसृतमन्दमन्दाकिनी   247

वक्रः पन्था यदपि भवतः प्रस्थितस्योत्तराशां   248

अनाघ्रातं पुष्पं किसलयमलूनं करहे ——   249

न किल भवतां टेल्याः स्थानं गृहेऽभिमतं ततः   249

पातुं न प्रथमं व्यवस्यति जलमं युष्मास्वपीतेषु या   250

जीर्णा कन्या ततः किं सितममलपटं पट्टसूत्रं ततः किम्   250

एते ते कूहरेषु गद्गदनदद् गोदावरीवारयो   252

आमूलालोलधुली बहुलपरिमला लीढलोलालीमाला   252

विजयदुन्दुभिनां ययुर्णवा घनरवा नरवाहनसंपदः   253

संचारिणी दीपशिखेव रात्रौ   253

गगनं गगनाकारं सागरः सागरोपमः ।   254

आश्च्योतनं नु हरिचन्दनपल्लवानां   254

लिम्पतीव तमोऽङ्गानि वर्षतीवाञ्जनं नभः ।   255

आशा नाम नदी मनोरथजला तृष्णातरंगाकुला   256

त्वं जीवितं त्वमसि मे हृदयं द्वितीयं   256

उदेति पूर्वं कुसुमं ततः फलं   257

नेता प्रियतमा वाचः   257

न प्रमाणीकृतः पाणिः   257

कामं नृपाः सन्तु सहस्रशोऽन्ये   258

इदं विलासव्याजमनोहरं वपु-   258

उपोढरागेण विलोलतारकं   259

अभिनवमधुलोलुपस्त्वं   259

वज्रादपि कठोराणि मृदूनि कुसुमादपि ।   260

या निशा सर्वभूतानां तस्यां जागर्ति संयमी ।   260

दलति हृदयं गाढोद्वेगं द्विधा न तु भिद्यते   260

प्रसाद इव मूर्तस्ते   261

अहो खलभुजंगस्य   261

ग्रीवाभंगाभिरामं मुहुरनुपतति स्यन्दने बक्रदृष्टिम्   262

उदये सविता रक्तो रक्तश्चास्तमने तथा ।   262

स्त्रीणामशिक्षितपटुत्वममानुषीषु   262

अलंकाराः

★★★★★★★★★★★★★★★★★ THE END ★★★★★★★★★★★★★★★★★★

ORDERING INFORMATION: BOOKS BY DR. BHARAT SHAH

⊙ **ENGLISH FOR THE GRANDMA AND HER CHILDREN.** $ 15.00 each.
A stepwise course (in Gujarati) for those who do not know any English. Written in simple, easy to read style, in large types, for students of any age to learn English at their own pace. No rules, conjugations, or declensions to memorize. Includes a glossary and a list of commonly used phrases to facilitate communication during a stay in a hospital. Approx. 200 pages.

⊙ **A PROGRAMMED TEXT TO LEARN GUJARATI (2nd Edition).** $20.00 each.
The thoroughly revised one volume second edition of a very popular three part self-study classic (in English), adopted as standard text book by several teachers. Ideal for the new generation of Gujaratis, ten years and up, born and brought up in the U.S.A. and elsewhere, to help them learn to read and write in Gujarati. Approx. 300 pages.

⊙ **AN INTRODUCTION TO JAINISM (Second Edition)** $ 18.00 each.
Electronicaly produced 7 X 10" slightly smaller type version of the highly acclaimed first edition. Treasure Chest, Glossary, and Index are thoroughly revised. The content is otherwise preserved. **Also available on <www.booksurge.com>**

⊙ **AN INTRODUCTION TO JAINISM (First Edition).** $ 15.00 each.
A highly acclaimed, simple introduction to Jainism (in English), especially for the new generation of Jains, written in a clear and friendly style, full of explanations, and a gradual, stepwise presentation of the fundamental principles. For personal or classroom study. Equally interesting for non Jains of either Indian or Western origin, and for students and scholars of non-violence, vegetarianism, and ecology. Approx. 200 pages, 8.5 x 11". Only while the supply lasts. Call to check for availability.

⊙ **A CRASH COURSE TO LEARN THE GUJARATI SCRIPT.** $ 03.00 each.

⊙ **A CRASH COURSE TO LEARN THE DEVANAGARI SCRIPT**
(for HINDI, MARATHI, AND SANSKRIT LANGUAGES). $ 03.00 each.
A very concise introduction, only about 20 pages long, to Gujarati or Devanagari scripts (in English), ideal for the American friends and sons- and daughters in law. One can learn to write one's own name, and that of one's family members, in a matter of couple of hours.

⊙ *SANSKRIT. AN APPRECIATION WITHOUT APPREHENSION.* $ 20.00 each.
For those who love Sanskrit, but are turned off by its complicated grammar. An introduction to the delightful language of scriptures and classical literature, and the mother of our mother tongues. Understand and appreciate all the classics, prayers and Subhashitani without any pain of remembering the complex rules. Covers the alphabet and grammar in a painless and innovative way. Appr. 300 pages.

⊙ **"SAMEEPE". AN EXPERIENCE BASED NOVEL IN GUJARATI.** $ 10.00 each.
An excellent autobiographical delightful saga of a supposedly painful experience of awaiting a liver transplant. Full of creative expressions, insightful observations, and gallows humor, with an undercurrent of sheer optimism.

    ⊙ *PRICE AND DISCOUNT (Prepaid oreders only)*
        1-9   books   No discount
        11   books, and more   Pay for ten, get one free
    ⊙ *SALES TAX* New York State residents add 8.5 % to the amount.
    ⊙ *SHIPPING AND HANDLING (Within the U.S.A.)*
        $ 2.00   for single copy of any Crash Course.
        $ 3.00   for any other book, plus $ 1for each additional book.
        $ 12.00   per every eleven books or a fraction thereof.
(TO ORDER ANY OF THE ABOVE PLEASE USE THE ORDER FORM ON THE OTHER SIDE)

ORDER FORM

Please review the information given on the other side carefully before preparing this order form. Check below the items that you wish to order. All orders must be accompanied by payment.

	TITLES	PRICE	NUMBER		AMOUNT
❑	**English** for the Grandma and Her Children	$15.00	X..............	=	$....................
❑	A Programmed Text to Learn **Gujarati**	$20.00	....		$....................
❑	An Introduction to **Jainism** (2nd Ed)	$18.00	....		$....................
❑	An Introduction to **Jainism** (1st Ed)	$15.00	....		$....................
❑	A Crash Course To Learn **The Gujarati Script**	$03.00	....		$....................
❑	A Crash Course To Learn **The Devanagari Script**	$03.00	....		$....................
❑	**Sanskrit.** An Appreciation Without Apprehension.	$20.00	....		$....................
❑	**"Sameepe".** A Novel in Gujarati.	$10.00	....		$....................

Sub Total $....................

Sales Tax 8.5 % of the sub total
  (New York State Residents only) $....................

Shipping and Handling $....................

GRAND TOTAL (Payable to Bharat S. Shah) $....................
(For Credit Card orders, please go to <www.amazon.com>

SHIP THE ORDER TO (Please Print Clearly):

Name:..

Address:..

City....................................State............Zip................-..............

Country......................Phone # (.........) ....-......................

Bharat S. Shah, M.D.
1 Lawson Lane
Great Neck, NY. 11023-1042. U.S.A.
(516)   482-6938.

ORDERING INFORMATION: BOOKS BY DR. BHARAT SHAH

⊘ **ENGLISH FOR THE GRANDMA AND HER CHILDREN.** **$ 15.00 each.**

A stepwise course (in Gujarati) for those who do not know any English. Written in simple, easy to read style, in large types, for students of any age to learn English at their own pace. No rules, conjugations, or declensions to memorize. Includes a glossary and a list of commonly used phrases to facilitate communication during a stay in a hospital. Approx. 200 pages.

⊘ **A PROGRAMMED TEXT TO LEARN GUJARATI (2nd Edition).** **$20.00 each.**

The thoroughly revised one volume second edition of a very popular three part self-study classic (in English), adopted as standard text book by several teachers. Ideal for the new generation of Gujaratis, ten years and up, born and brought up in the U.S.A. and elsewhere, to help them learn to read and write in Gujarati. Approx. 300 pages.

⊘ **AN INTRODUCTION TO JAINISM (Second Edition)** **$ 18.00 each.**

Electronicaly produced 7 X 10" slightly smaller type version of the highly acclaimed first edition. Treasure Chest, Glossary, and Index are thoroughly revised. The content is otherwise preserved. **Also available on <www.booksurge.com>**

⊘ **AN INTRODUCTION TO JAINISM (First Edition).** **$ 15.00 each.**

A highly acclaimed, simple introduction to Jainism (in English), especially for the new generation of Jains, written in a clear and friendly style, full of explanations, and a gradual, stepwise presentation of the fundamental principles. For personal or classroom study. Equally interesting for non Jains of either Indian or Western origin, and for students and scholars of non-violence, vegetarianism, and ecology. Approx. 200 pages, 8.5 x 11". Only while the supply lasts. Call to check for availability.

⊘ **A CRASH COURSE TO LEARN THE GUJARATI SCRIPT.** **$ 03.00 each.**

⊘ **A CRASH COURSE TO LEARN THE DEVANAGARI SCRIPT**
(for HINDI, MARATHI, AND SANSKRIT LANGUAGES). **$ 03.00 each.**

A very concise introduction, only about 20 pages long, to Gujarati or Devanagari scripts (in English), ideal for the American friends and sons- and daughters in law. One can learn to write one's own name, and that of one's family members, in a matter of couple of hours.

⊘ *SANSKRIT. AN APPRECIATION WITHOUT APPREHENSION.* **$ 20.00 each.**

For those who love Sanskrit, but are turned off by its complicated grammar. An introduction to the delightful language of scriptures and classical literature, and the mother of our mother tongues. Understand and appreciate all the classics, prayers and Subhashitani without any pain of remembering the complex rules. Covers the alphabet and grammar in a painless and innovative way. Appr. 300 pages.

⊘ **"SAMEEPE". AN EXPERIENCE BASED NOVEL IN GUJARATI.** **$ 10.00 each.**

An excellent autobiographical delightful saga of a supposedly painful experience of awaiting a liver transplant. Full of creative expressions, insightful observations, and gallows humor, with an undercurrent of sheer optimism.

     ⊘ *PRICE AND DISCOUNT (Prepaid oreders only)*

         1-9   books   No discount

         11   books, and more   Pay for ten, get one free

     ⊘ *SALES TAX* New York State residents add 8.5 % to the amount.

     ⊘ *SHIPPING AND HANDLING (Within the U.S.A.)*

         $ 2.00   for single copy of any Crash Course.

         $ 3.00   for any other book, plus $ 1for each additional book.

         $ 12.00   per every eleven books or a fraction thereof.

(TO ORDER ANY OF THE ABOVE PLEASE USE THE ORDER FORM ON THE OTHER SIDE)

ORDER FORM

Please review the information given on the other side carefully before preparing this order form. Check below the items that you wish to order. All orders must be accompanied by payment.

	TITLES	PRICE	NUMBER	AMOUNT
❏	**English** for the Grandma and Her Children	$15.00	X............. =	$....................
❏	A Programmed Text to Learn **Gujarati**	$20.00	....	$....................
❏	An Introduction to **Jainism** (2nd Ed)	$18.00	....	$....................
❏	An Introduction to **Jainism** (1st Ed)	$15.00	....	$....................
❏	A Crash Course To Learn **The Gujarati Script**	$03.00	....	$....................
❏	A Crash Course To Learn **The Devanagari Script**	$03.00	....	$....................
❏	**Sanskrit.** An Appreciation Without Apprehension.	$20.00	....	$....................
❏	**"Sameepe".** A Novel in Gujarati.	$10.00	....	$....................
	Sub Total			$....................
	Sales Tax 8.5 % of the sub total (New York State Residents only)			$....................
	Shipping and Handling			$....................
	GRAND TOTAL (Payable to Bharat S. Shah) (For Credit Card orders, please go to <www.amazon.com>			$....................

SHIP THE ORDER TO *(Please Print Clearly):*

Name:...

Address:...

City.................................State............Zip................-.............

Country.....................Phone # (.........) ....-.......................

Bharat S. Shah, M.D.
1 Lawson Lane
Great Neck, NY. 11023-1042. U.S.A.
(516) 482-6938.

21223004R00154

Made in the USA
Lexington, KY
04 March 2013